NEXT

**Thoughts about tomorrow
you can talk about today**

Matt Church

th⊚ught leaders

Published by Thought Leaders Publishing

First published 2017
Reprinted 2018
This edition 2022

Thought Leaders Publishing
2B, 3-9 Kenneth Street
Manly Vale NSW 2093

ISBN: 978 0 9874708-6-7

Editing by Michelle Phillips
Design & typesetting by Michael Fink
Produced for the publisher by exlibris.com.au

Contents

ABOUT
THE AUTHOR

Matt Church is the founder of Thought Leaders and a strategic thinker, obsessed with the idea of leverage. While many are painting a scary view of the future he sees one full of potential. Whether it's what he writes, his advice to thought leaders or his extraordinary conference presentations; he communicates with deep focus, commercial clarity and a razor sharp wit. His work focuses on three things: removing fear and replacing it with confidence, removing confusion and replacing with certainty and mobilising people in pursuit of a better future.

FOREWORD

Funnily enough I want to start this foreword by looking backwards.

15,000 years ago we were all hunter-gathers. While census data wasn't kept all that accurately back then, we do know there were less than 10 million of us on the planet — less people than there are in Chicago today.

In his book, *Sapiens*, Yuval Noah Harari makes the compelling argument that while the transition from hunting and gathering to farming was good for the species, it actually didn't make life better for individuals. In fact he calls the agricultural revolution "history's biggest fraud" and writes that farmers generally had lives that were more difficult and less satisfying than foragers.

We definitely ended up with more food, but that didn't result in a better diet or more leisure. Just more people, working longer hours, with a more homogeneous diet.

The last one hundred and fifty years tells a similar story.

One hundred and fifty years ago there were a little more than a billion of us on the planet.

Seventy five per cent of the working population in the USA in 1870 was involved in food production. Today it is under two per cent (and according to the Australian Bureau of Statistics these numbers are similar in Australia).

iv | **NEXT**

It would be an interesting exercise to sit down with a town of a hundred workers back in the day — a hundred and fifty years ago — and design how work would look if only two of them were now needed to produce the food for the whole town.

The conversation would start by saying "We now have 73 of us that are free to do whatever we decide. Perhaps everyone should just work a quarter of the time. What else would we want to do? Or maybe we should work a bit more than that and acquire more stuff."

We could ask who wants a bigger house. Someone might say an extra room would be nice — get the kids sleeping in a different room. (We've actually made houses ten times bigger despite there being no evidence that there is a correlation between bigger houses and more happiness.)

We might ask who wants some more clothes. Our townsfolk might have answered that another shirt would be nice, and new shoes for the kids too. (Many of us now actually have a whole room just for our clothes, and still have so many clothes that they won't all fit in the space.)

Apart from having a lot bigger houses filled with much more stuff, what are we actually doing with all this time that's been freed up? What are the 73 people out of every hundred who are no longer producing food doing?

Out of every 100 workers today in the USA:

- 15 are the government. (15 people to govern the other 85? Yep.)

- 13 are in mining, construction and manufacturing, making all the stuff.

- 18 are selling the stuff to everyone else.

- 12 are in healthcare.

- 10 are in leisure and hospitality.

- A couple are in education teaching everyone else how all this works.

- Another 18 are basically having meetings and writing emails (information, financial activities, professional and business services).

- And the other 12 will be doing other. It's not exactly clear what that is, but I'm sure it involves meetings and emails.

Despite it taking less than two per cent of the population now to feed us all, and having the opportunity to design our lives and our societies to look pretty much however we want, we're actually working harder than ever, and are no happier than we were 150 years ago.

If that sounds kind of nuts, it's because it is.

With the convergence of artificial intelligence, automation and globalisation the next fifteen years promises to see change of a similar order of magnitude to the last one hundred and fifty years … or to the 15,000 years before that. And again, despite the massive opportunity that this will present for us, there is no guarantee that this will actually make things better.

Our evolution over the last million years means we're set up to survive in the savannah of Africa much more than to thrive in this brave new world. At an individual and organisational level we're not set up to design a life or an organisation that works in the face of change of this magnitude.

Over the last two decades Matt Church has put together a body of work unparalleled by any other business thinker, speaker or author in the world. In this book he has addressed how we need to think and what we need to do to take advantage of this next phase of history.

In *Next* Matt has curated some of the best ideas on the planet, and more importantly shared his own thinking, in a brilliant format.

The ideas and program outlined in this book will not only help you thrive in the decade of disruption, they will also will also help you bring your team and organisation along for the ride.

Peter Cook, *CEO Thought Leaders*

INTRODUCTION

This book is written with the busy leader in mind. With so many books published each day, you don't have time to read them all. And that's probably not even the right goal. Leaders have to spend a lot of time taking care of the day-to-day in their businesses. With this in mind, I decided to start sharing short essays around ideas that I think are worth discussing. Each month I'd publish these articles on various platforms and give leaders something to discuss with their teams that went beyond the day-to-day.

The topics are broad ranging, but focus on ideas that can leverage our time and talents, to get more done in less time and to future-proof our careers, businesses and teams. Compiling these ideas into a book was a natural next step.

Each chapter is set up as an idea that should generate some conversation, create some distinctions, suggest some possible novel insights, and result in a team decision. A decision to try something new, change something old, or explore an idea that makes performing at your best easier.

The book is a program, not one you need to invest hundreds of thousands of dollars to apply, but one you can run in-house, by yourself. Maybe you want to set up a Lunch and Learn.

Use the book to get your mind racing, sign up as a 'Next Leader' online and use the resources provided to make a difference in your organisation.

I have built and run some extraordinary change programs throughout my years, but have come to realise that often it's the people within the business who are the real agents of change and that their actions often have the best chance of making a difference to the business.

I promise to do my part and curate the ideas; let's see what you can do to make shift happen from here.

M@

Beyond Reading

If you want to lead a discussion around some of these chapters here is what I suggest:

1. Chat one-on-one with major team members socialising the ideas. Draw the models on a napkin or coaster, and have a couple of the discussion ideas in mind as you do this.

2. Set up a Book Club meeting and bounce the ideas around with people (3–5 people). Register as a Next Leader and get the mailable PDFs of chapters.

3. Lead a Lunch and Learn (5–15 people) with your team. Register as a Next Leader and download the slide decks so that the discussion is smooth and organised.

It's easy to register as a Next Leader. Simply register online at thoughtleaders.com.au/next to become a Facilitator, agreeing to the creative commons licence agreement, at no cost to you. Then you are ready to start having meaningful discussions around each chapter.

Suggested Process

Step 1
Circulate one chapter at a time. Each chapter is available online as a sharable PDF for anyone who registers as a leader. You can email these to your team members or clients.

Step 2
Download the facilitator's guide and read it, practising drawing any models or diagrams in stages as a context setter.

Step 3
Set up a meeting to discuss the chapter and its relevance to what you and your team are doing. Facilitate a short discussion about the ideas in the chapter using the questions in the facilitator's guide.

Step 4
Share your experience and tips to our online 'Leaders' platform.

Step 5
If you like the ideas and would like Matt to bring them alive at your next company conference then simply email hello@mattchurch.com

THE DECADE OF DISRUPTION

Change creeps up on us. There is a unapologetic focus in each of these chapters towards the future. More accurately, a focus on what can you do today to impact tomorrow. This chapter will tackle the imperative of getting okay with disruption. It's time to realise we are firmly wedged in the decade of disruption.

This is an age of unprecedented change. Revolution and disruption transform the world almost daily. Ideas that seemed fanciful in science fiction novels only decades ago are now a physical reality we often take for granted.

The idea that 4.77 billion people would own a mobile phone in 2017 would have seemed ridiculous in the mid-1980s, when that was the total number of people on the planet. You keep a device in your pocket that can deliver satellite imagery of any location on earth with the touch of a finger. Imagine what the armies of the past would have given for that kind of information! You can remotely fly a drone purchased for less than $1000, or take super-slow motion video that was the domain of professional equipment costing well into six figures only a decade ago.

We have a choice to become agents for change, amplifiers, and thought leaders; to upgrade our thinking and lead our tribes into new and exciting futures.

All of this can be done with consumer equipment available to all living in anything other than abject poverty. One imagines that Isaac Asimov — perhaps the greatest futurist of the 20th century — would be both shocked and amazed.

We live in the exponential age. It's not just that change is happening quickly; the rate of change itself is increasing at exponentially increasing rates. Products, jobs, companies — and indeed whole industries — are being made redundant. As we look back on the last 200 years, the most transformative period in the history of humankind, it's sobering to recognise that for all that changed over that period, the coming decade might surpass it. The next decade will be the most unpredictable decade in history. It will be the most productive decade in history. It will be, arguably, the most exciting decade in history. It will certainly be the most disruptive decade in history (see Figure 1 on page 3).

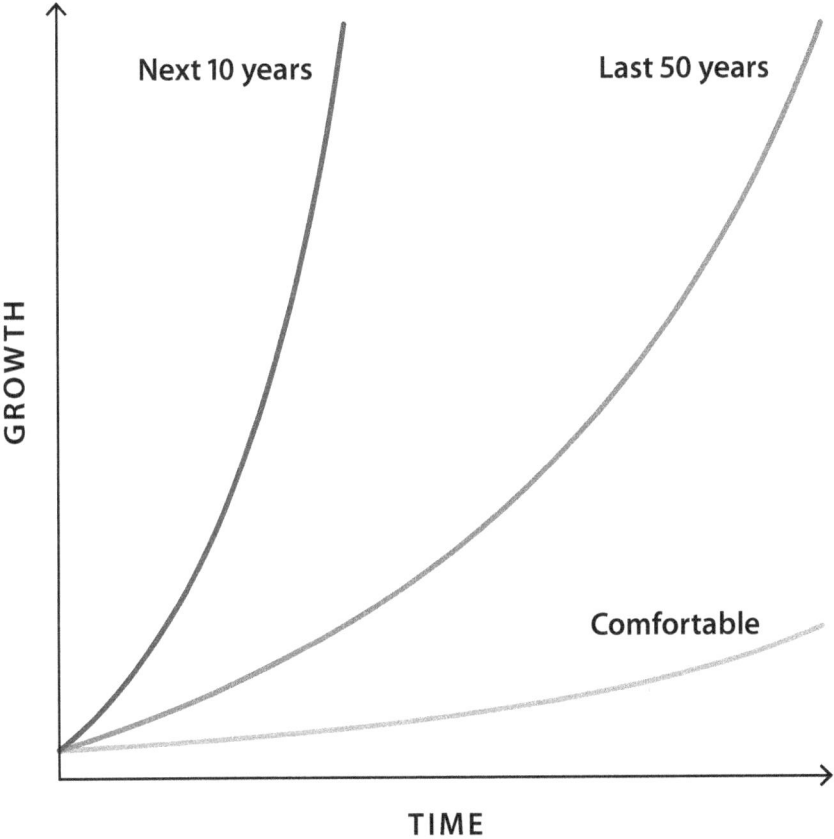

Figure 1. Pace of change accelerating

This is a fascinating idea, and it raises many questions. How do we respond to it? How do we react? How do we evolve to keep ourselves relevant? How do we guide our children and best prepare them for the uncertain future? How do we structure our companies to give them the best chance of success?

Contrary to the expressed opinions of many futurists, humans like change. Change is called progress if it's in your best interests and something you feel is in your control. The first line on this explores the comfortable, organic change of progress.

The last 50 years have seen massive change and disruption, and it doesn't look like it's slowing down. Most agree that the next decade or so will see change accelerating at an extreme rate, the curve will lick up, looking like the curve in a hockey stick. At the time of writing, the biggest accommodation business owns no property, the biggest taxi business has no cars, the biggest retailer has no inventory and the biggest content platform produces no content.

The next decade will be the most unpredictable decade in history. It will be the most productive decade in history. It will be, arguably, the most exciting decade in history. It will certainly be the most disruptive decade in history.

The well known phrase 'may you live in interesting times' is right here, right now. Just as the horseshoe market was made redundant by Henry Ford, people in industries from accounting to zoology are being put out of work because the work they do is no longer in demand. Businesses are shutting down because a start-up not only took their customers away but completely reconfigured their market. Power is shifting, fast. It's shifting from seller to buyer, from information to insight, from employer to employee, from strategy to culture. It's shifting from authoritative, formal leaders to inspiring, informal ones. The world is moving so fast that we are educating children for jobs that have not yet been conceived to solve problems that don't yet exist.

The next decade will likely see China surpass the US for gross domestic product, the number of millionaires, and the number of English speaking citizens. The G7 will be replaced not only by the BRICS economies, but also chased through the following decades by the emerging economies of Africa, Vietnam, and many other non-traditional power houses. This wholesale change could be perceived as a threat. It can also be framed as an incredible opportunity.

We have more choice than ever before, and yet we are more exhausted than we have ever been. We are more connected than ever before and yet feel more isolated, lonely, and discontent.

People have evolved to exist most comfortably in the status quo. We like to feel secure and safe in a known and predictable environment. As a result, we tend to experience change as an unwelcome interruption — a revolution. It's a perspective that frames the coming decade as a period of uncomfortable and unwanted disruption. In this book, I hope to promote the idea that it is a call to personal growth, an invitation to transformation — an evolution. I am in no way trying to predict the landscape of business and life in ten years' time (who would be so foolish as to try?), but I am interested in developing the mindsets, capabilities and cultures that will thrive in the world of Tomorrowland (see Figure 2 on page 6).

This is one of the greatest times to be alive. By all objective measures, it's better to be an average woman today than a queen in eras past. We live longer, healthier lives. We are safer, more secure, and more self-actualised than ever before. However we could hardly be said to be living in utopia just yet.

REVOLUTION	EVOLUTION
Challenges the past	Invested in the future
Reactive	Proactive
Antagonist	Protagonist
Fear-based	Inspirational
Fighter	Enlightener
Takes	Gives
Believes in 'wrong'	Believes in 'better'
Destructive	Creative
Victim mentality	Visionary
Win – Lose	Win – Well

Acknowledgement:
Michael Henderson, The Corporate Anthropologist

Figure 2. Revolution versus Evolution Distinctions

We have more choice than ever before, and yet we are more exhausted than we have ever been. We are more connected than ever before and yet feel more isolated, lonely, and discontent.

In this age of self-determination, designing your life and starting a personal evolution is no longer a nice idea or a luxury, it's the critical next step. This is so much more than work-life balance; it's about an intentional act of creation. You don't discover who you are — you create who you are.

It's a professional evolution!

Large organisations are feeling the effects of disruption and it's far beyond the buzzwords and phrases, so much more than 'generational mindsets' or 'employee engagement'.

Big business needs to meet in smarter ways, engage customers with authenticity and develop an agility that their cultures resist. 'Change management' is dead, it's time to lead through disruption. The world is not as simple as we tried to make it; this is about influence, not communication, it's about standing out, not fitting in, it's about resourcefulness and execution.

The professional evolution demands of you one simple thing; that you become an agent of change. The enemy is status quo. Your business needs you to lead fearlessly and transparently, willing to try new things and both succeed and fail in public.

It's an entrepreneurial evolution!

It's easy to see how new businesses are often the revolutionaries. Stories of Zappos and Google have become seminar clichés; the entrepreneurial spirit is one that revolutionaries can embrace and hold a torch up to. The spirit of an entrepreneur is about declaring war on the conceptual enemy of progress — sameness! It's time we put the status quo on notice.

Are you up for leading the next evolution?

Can you start a peaceful revolution? Are you nimble enough, charismatic enough to become an agent of change? Are you willing to put in the work to become a thought leader? Will you take charge of your life, your career, your business and make a difference? If you are not leading the evolution, you are being disrupted.

Each of us is faced with a challenge. Will we lead the tide of change in our business and personal lives, or will we play catch-up? We all have a choice to step up into personal, professional and social leadership. We have a choice to become agents for change, amplifiers, and thought leaders; to upgrade our thinking and lead our tribes into new and exciting futures.

Calling oneself a futurist in a world where predicting the future is a mathematical impossibility is a dangerous game to say the least.

The intent of this book is not, therefore, to paint an accurate prediction of the decade ahead. Indeed, I fully expect every mention of possible futures in this book to be disproved at some point in the next ten years; and in those rare cases where I'm proven to be correct, I'll happily credit the result to random chance.

The laggards in the decade of disruption will be the losers of the era to follow.

My intention is not to amaze and delight your imagination with science fiction. It is not to give you the inspiration for the next great app or to put a flagpole in the centre of the next industry to be irreparably disrupted. Instead, my goal is to give you some practical tools you can implement in your business and your life to help put you at the forefront of the wave to the next. The laggards in the decade of disruption will be the losers of the era to follow.

I understand that rarely do professionals have time to sit and digest an entire book in one sitting. I'm quite happy for this book to become your companion on the commode, and each time you make a small deposit to the local sewer, you can make a small investment in your future productivity.

This book is full of thought starters; ideas I have about Tomorrowland, musings and practical suggestions for how you might adapt, react and respond in this the decade of disruption.

Each chapter is designed to stand alone, interlinked and yet individually useful.

DISCUSSION IDEAS

1 Name the biggest disruption ideas, businesses or events of the last 50 years?

_____

_____

_____

2 What do you think of Airbnb, Uber and YouTube?

_____

_____

_____

3 What nations are likely to emerge as the next economic powerhouses after the BRICS nations?

_____

_____

_____

4 Are you an agent of change? If so, what do you do that's different than an 'employee'?

_____

_____

_____

5 What are the social trends that impact your business right now?

_____
_____
_____

6 What are the technological trends that impact your business right now?

_____
_____
_____

7 What are the economic trends that impact your business right now?

_____
_____
_____

8 What are the environmental trends that impact your business right now?

_____
_____
_____

9 What are the political issues that impact your business right now?

_____
_____
_____

2

REINVENTING READING

This chapter is about encouraging people to read. However, busy leaders are already struggling to stay on top of their professional reading, let alone adding more to this! We need to reinvent the way we read. The very structure of this book is designed to make your reading task easier. This chapter will delve further into how to process written content in a way that is useful, efficient, and enjoyable.

Do you read non-fiction books? My son remarked the other day about the similarity of the titles of the books I read. I explained the genre to him and, while agreeing that they sounded the same, pointed out that they were about different topics. I see them as mentoring lessons; ideas picked up from others' hard work that I could use in life and business to make progress, change or money.

At around my son's age, I committed to a life of continuous improvement. A copy of Brian Tracy's *Psychology of Achievement* audio tapes, left behind by an Amway salesperson, set me on a path of personal development, and today books are still my favourite way to learn. The impersonal, yet intimate, nature of reading is something I have treasured for decades.

Here are some thoughts on hacking books, reading more, and reinventing how you read.

I read a lot and still don't feel like I can keep up with all there is to learn. It doesn't make me anxious, I'm just excited about the possibilities. My business (thought leadership) demands that I be well read and my occupation (public speaking) means that I need to stay fit and healthy, but in both cases that professional imperative does not directly translate to me eating well enough or reading enough. I fight daily to stay well, and I fight to stay well read. I imagine it's the same for you?

Here are some thoughts on hacking books, reading more, and reinventing how you read.

Statistics suggest that there are about 3000 books published a day — perhaps more. That means if you were to read a book a day for the next ten years, you would only be able to read the books that came out today. Keeping up is not the goal. Being well informed is.

Warren Buffet, when asked what was the key to his success, pointed to a pile of non-fiction books and stated "Read 500 pages like this every day. That's how knowledge works. It builds up, like compound interest. All of you can do it, but I guarantee not many of you will do it." Andrew Merle unpacks this idea in greater detail in his Huffington post article The Reading Habits of Ultra-Successful People.[1]

A great blogger I follow is Charlie Chu, who publishes under the name betterhumans.com. He does some great maths in his post around how to read 500 pages a day.[2] The bottom line is that most people spend more time on social media watching cat videos than they do reading. That's a sobering thought.

Nikolai Goeie Made is keen to help people develop the habit of reading. He summarises books for a living and so certainly has a vested interest. In his article Time2Read he talks about how to develop the reading habit, especially when you think you don't have time.[3]

> *Keeping up is not the goal. Being well informed is.*

What have we learnt from those thoughts above?

You need to read. It's one of the things very successful people have in common. Reading well and widely expands your potential, and then helps you reach it. Good readers gain knowledge, deepen their ideas, and are exposed to different points of views. This is a vital building block for success.

You do have the time. The way we used to read may not serve us anymore, because 'Life gets in the way'. Books sit untouched on our bedside table, or unopened on our book shelves. Our intentions may be good, but we rarely find the time to actually turn the pages. Like exercise, we know reading is good for us, and yet still we don't do it. So, like exercise, reading needs to become a habit, a ritual, part of your daily pattern.

Here are five ideas you might find useful to help you reinvent your reading habit.

You're not qualified to choose the books you read

You can't visit every hotel in the world to determine which one to stay at. You use travel bloggers, magazines and Trip Advisor to help you sift through which hotel in Amalfi or villa in Como you book. Delegate the process of picking which books to read to smarter people than you. Bottom line — we are not qualified to choose what books we read.

If you are old enough to remember book stores, you know the joy of losing yourself in one, flicking through available books and picking one to read, often swayed by cover design and catchy titles. Now that the book store is a rarity, we have an unintended positive consequence — books are judged by their content, not their covers. It's a good thing. Find some qualified people you admire and tap into their reading list. Let them do the heavy lifting for you. Goodreads is a great place to start and so are the annual lists by famous people. I like Bill Gates' annual reading list.[4] I also regularly ask people "What's a great book you have read recently?" I write down recommendations religiously, halting conversations until I have captured the suggestion or actually searched it on Amazon, often purchasing it mid conversation.

Read the right book at the right time

I reckon there are different ways to read and different types of reading. I divide my books into three categories: Adrenaline, Academic and Anaesthetic (see Figure 3 on page 17).

The Adrenaline (On) books are how I often start my day or find new energy and inspiration during the day. The Academic (Up) books are used as reference tools while I work. Both of these are

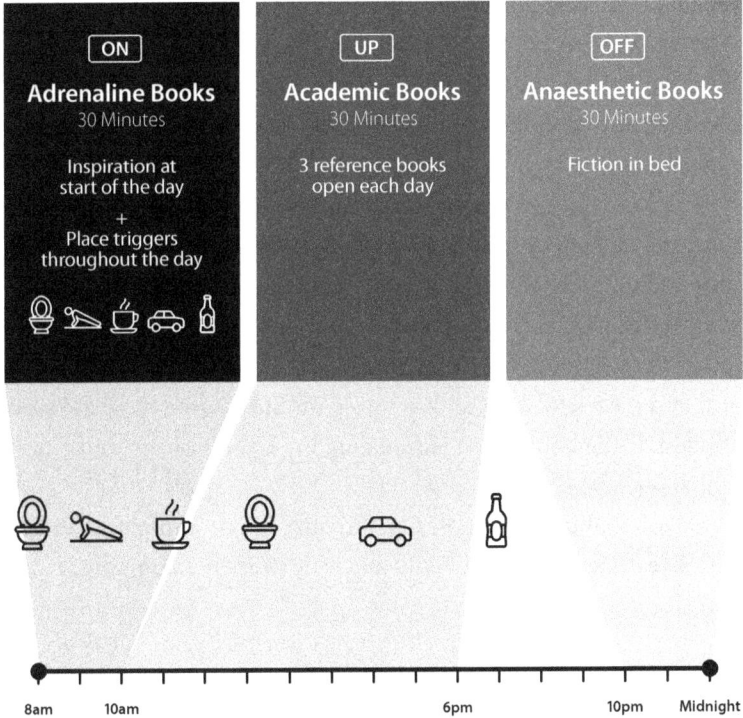

Figure 3.   A good reading day

non-fiction. Meanwhile, I keep my Anaesthetic (Off) books, which are fiction, for the night or at the end of a tough day, save for an occasional little treat at lunch.

I read them differently as well. An Off book gets read with the mindlessness of watching a movie — I identify with characters, sub-vocalise, visualise, and get caught up in the descriptive language. Whereas the On books are read actively, constantly asking myself 'What do I think about that?' The Up books are studied slowly and methodically, and dissected forensically, cross-referencing one idea with the next.

You can organise yourself to get things done four different ways; time, place, project and people. When it comes to reading, I think time and place are the most effective contexts. I have a slightly addic-tive personality and so 'chain smoke' books. If I let myself, I will read rather than work, so the 'what book when' divisions are significant. I also find it hard to sleep, and so I need discipline around what I read at night. If the book is too stimulating my brain kicks in and I can't switch off.

So adrenalin in the morning and anaesthetic at night, with aca-demic reads as required to build a case or strengthen opinion.

IDEA 3

Don't 'read' books, absorb them

A book takes too long to read, and the staring at a screen or wading through pages in an actual book can be a little counter productive. Discipline and will power aside, maybe you also need to find a better way to read.

Originally written in 1940 and first published by Simon & Schus-ter in 1972, *How to Read a Book* introduces and elucidates the various levels of reading and how to achieve them to gain the most under-standing and insight from any book. Make this the first Blink you read today (see Idea 4, below) after downloading the app.

It's the business books I need to read that pileup. Several years ago I adopted the rule that each book gets a one-hour sitting. I sit down and pull it apart. I don't start reading at the beginning or enrol in a speed reading course, I just intentionally flick through it trying to get what it's about. I read the first ten pages; I read the table of contents, I study diagrams. I read the chapter summaries if they have them and typically in the hour, I can fit in one chapter, which I read from start to finish. The first 40 minutes are choosing which chapter gets the full read treatment. At the end of this process, I decide whether the book deserves more time. If so, it gets moved into the queue, but I am pretty ruthless!

What's interesting is the conversations that my kids have about each book they see move in and out of the bathrooms.

Three that made it through to the full read queue this year were *Antifragile* by Nicolas Taleb, *Smartcuts* by Shane Snow and *Big Magic* by Elisabeth Gilbert.

IDEA 4

Set place triggers to help you develop the reading habit

Apps and summary services help you absorb books faster. I use apps and summary services to help me triage the ideas and concepts in books. I also use them in different places and on different devices. Blinkist is on my phone (and only on my phone) and means I can read a book in five minutes in the cracks between life. Often when I'm about to check social media, I stop and read a Blink first. GetAbstract sends PDF summaries that can be read in 15 minutes. I only do these on iPad, and it's when I have a coffee by myself. Audible gives you a spoken summary that you can listen to when in cars. I don't do this so much anymore (Blinkist has replaced it), but for those who drive alone a lot, this is gold.

The 'place' triggers help you make a habit of reading. I choose three Up (Academic) reference books to sit on my desk each working day. Usually a current best seller (published within last 12 months), a contemporary best seller (three years old or so) and a classic (more than ten years old). These are curated based on what my current primary work question — 'What's the one thing I need to achieve today?' Because my days are structured contextually (Sales, Leadership, etc.) this is probably a bit easier for me than some others.

A book that lends itself to bitesize pieces gets placed in one of the two bathrooms I regularly use at home and chunks are read while sitting on the loo. Three that made it through to my 'Dunny list': Alan De Botton's *Religion for Atheists*, *Rework* By Jason Fried and *Rules for Revolutionaries* by Guy Kawasaki. Quick, self-contained chapters that you can read in one sitting, literally. (That should stop anyone wanting to borrow those!)

What's interesting is the conversations that my kids have about each book they see move in and out of the bathrooms. Often they have picked them up, flicked through them, and will ask me to summarise the book. Smart kids, they have outsourced the reading to their dad!

Do something with the knowledge quickly

Edward De Bono once wrote that if smoking turned your skin orange immediately, fewer people would smoke. Consequences that are divorced from the action often don't motivate change. Same with books. Reading a book may earn you Buffet's compound interest, but it's delayed. What's the quick fix pay-off to reading? Well, there isn't one, so you have to make one up. It's why books clubs work. They are reading boot camps; each member knows they better have read the book or they will look like an idiot.

Not one for clubs, I need something more individualistic. I try to pass the idea on. Easy for me when I am on stage, or on webcasts, or writing books or blog posts, but we can all do it. In general conversation — "Hey, I read a cool book the other day that shared (insert idea). What do you think of that?" — or in an email sent to client or colleague — "Read this in book X and thought you might find useful!" — Or send the team you manage an email with the key takeaways of the book you just read. It doesn't matter how you share, but the principle of having to use the idea quickly gives it a reason to be read.

Read the right book at the right time

Final thoughts on the future of books

The publishing industry is in a spin, undergoing many changes. The fabulous Seth Godin once said that he believes the future of books will be as souvenirs. Some of the books I have read I want to own. Maybe as trophies of my accomplishment, but more as memory joggers and quick references. Besides, I love the look of a New York loft floor-to-ceiling bookcase. And who hasn't lost themselves in a great bookshelf for a few hours?

It's a bit like children of the last decade who may never see photos of themselves. Their parents transitioned from print to digital and so, instead of boxes full of snapshots of dad with a cool car and mum in a swish outfit, we have hard drives full of memory (literally).

I plan to buy the best form of the books I loved; big hardcopy, velum-bound, gold lettering, signed-by-the-author versions. That means I often buy my favourite books several times; firstly on a subscription service like Get Abstract or Blinkist, then $9 for the digital version and finally $90 for the gorgeous collector's edition. Maybe digital is not lowering the cost of books but rather increasing it, along with a whole lot of other good things.

Oh, we have got to print some photos of the kids, just the good ones mind you (photos that is, not kids). But when we do, we need to frame them, gild them, and make more of them — ah hell I reckon I just signed up for scrapbooking! Explains why scrapbooking is a fast growing trend though doesn't it!

ONLINE REFERENCES

1. Andrew Merle. 2016. *The Reading Habits of Ultra-Successful People.*
    http://www.huffingtonpost.com/andrew-merle/the-reading-habits-of-
    ult_b_9688130.html

2. Charles Chu. 2017. *The Simple Truth Behind Reading 200 Books a Year.*
    https://betterhumans.coach.me/the-simple-truth-behind-reading-
    200-books-a-year-1767cb03af20

3. Nikolai Goeie Made. 2016. http://time2read.co/

4. Bill Gates. 2016. *My Favorite Books of 2016.*
    https://www.gatesnotes.com/About-Bill-Gates/Best-Books-2016

BOOKS MENTIONED

de Botton, A., 2012. *Religion for Atheists: A Non-Believer's Guide to the Uses of Religion.* 1st ed. United States: Pantheon Books.

Fried, J., 2010. *Rework.* 1st ed. United States: Crown Business.

Gilbert, E., 2016. *Big Magic: Creative Living Beyond Fear.* 1st ed. United States: Riverhead.

Kawasaki, G., 1999. *Rules For Revolutionaries: The Capitalist Manifesto for Creating and Marketing New Products and Services.* 1st ed. United States: HarperCollins.

Snow, S., 2014. *Smartcuts: The Breakthrough Power of Lateral Thinking.* 1st ed. United States: HarperCollins.

Taleb, N., 2012. *Antifragile: Things That Gain from Disorder.* 1st ed. United States: Random House.

DISCUSSION IDEAS

1 **What have you read lately?**

_____
_____
_____

2 **What place triggers could you set or adopt?**

_____
_____
_____

3 **How can you share an idea as you learn it?**

_____
_____
_____

4 **What's your reading goal?**

_____
_____
_____

5 **Who would be part of your professional book club?**

_____
_____
_____

6 What's the future of books?

_____

_____

_____

7 What are some new ways to gain knowledge, that don't require reading?

_____

_____

_____

3

CHANGEMONGERS

Change gets a bad wrap. It seems that many people are invested in the status quo. Keeping things the same wherever they can. I get it; change is a pain. It's why we hold off buying the new computer, phone, or updating to the latest operating system. Each time you change something it's like process steps get broken, our systems end up with holes in them. We need to incentivise change; this chapter is metaphorically suggesting that we can profit from change if we lead it rather than manage it.

Throughout history, there have been countless examples of warmongers; entrepreneurs and politicians who thrive in the disruption of war. Warmongers profit by selling arms, trading in human lives, and preying on the negative impacts these disruptive events create. As mercenary and unpleasant as the idea of warmongering is, perhaps it's the context of the behaviour (rather than the behaviour itself) that's distasteful.

Maybe the strategies mongers employed when profiting from war should be informing (to a point) the strategies we will employ in this decade of disruption. As we approach these revolutionary ten years — where primary business models are failing, industries are closing down, jobs are being reworked, and economic super powers are shifting like tectonic plates — you need to consciously position yourself for competitive advantage. You, as the internal thought leader for your business, need to be a *changemonger*.

To have this appetite for change, you need to make the act of change an imperative that you lead, rather than a process that you manage. You must be willing to swim upstream. You also need to act with a somewhat revolutionary intent. It's about being willing to take what is considered normal (and possibly sacred) and put it out to pasture in favour of what is necessary and new. This kind of change is difficult because it goes against the safe, normalising behaviour that got you to this point in the first place. As Dr Marshall Goldsmith said, "What got you here won't get you there." The problem with success is that it hardens your approach and causes you to repeat actions that worked in the past. If the speed of change is glacial, that's fine. When it more closely resembles an avalanche, maintaining the course that brought you past successes might result in future catastrophe.

You as the internal thought leader for your business need to be a change monger.

There are a few common difficulties all changemongers face. First, you need to recognise that the signals for change are absent if you are ahead of the curve. The absence of signals makes it challenging to convince others of the necessity for change, because they may not see the need until it's already too late. Second, you need to find some wriggle room to make a change outside of the system. Thirdly, you need to lead the emotions of stakeholders so that the change is experienced as an ideal evolution

> *The problem with success is that it hardens your approach and causes you to repeat actions that worked in the past.*

versus an aggressive revolution; we're not really at war here after all, and you need to motivate your people to come along with you.

There are three strategies you can employ to break down these barriers:

- *Make status quo the enemy.* People won't see the same need for change as you, so you need to wage a constant war on 'business as usual'.

- *Make embracing change a culture, not a strategy.* It will be hard to change a system from within it, so you need to create a culture for change in your organisation.

- *Make leadership the change imperative.* It needs to be an evolution that you lead, not a forced revolution.

Make status quo the enemy

"Amazon ate my server."

Amazon was looking after their own data-hosting needs when they developed all their server technology. One day they woke up and realised that they could sell their server space to other companies with similar requirements. There was a market for 'cloud' storage, and most importantly, what they had developed was faster and more flexible than what all the big status quo companies were offering.

Even the big names of technology can't stay the big names of technology when they don't move forwards aggressively. Dell, HP, EMC and Cisco provide servers, and Oracle and IBM offer databases. Amazon has made their traditional server technologies obsolete.[1] With the advent of Amazon Cloud, the business model of data management has been disrupted, as servers are now mostly free and there is open-source access to the programming that drives them. Even worse for these companies, Amazon is now going after their legacy customers — those feeling locked into a long term relationship based on the (deliberate?) inflexibility of the provided product. Clients who these companies thought untouchable are now given the opportunity to transfer their data to the Amazon Cloud with ease.

Business as usual is not going to help us adapt and thrive in the decade of disruption.

Business as usual is not going to help us adapt and thrive in the decade of disruption. It's about being able to see the next steps and navigate change before it's even begun to happen.

Take the Big 5 business ideas of the moment: information, innovation, efficiency, change and engagement, and you can see a dramatic shift in what they mean and what matters in each case (see Figure 4 on page 31). Things are not staying still long enough for old paradigms and out of date distinctions to have any relevance. The following table explains the shift in meaning around these issues. On the left is what they used to be about and on the right is what they need to be about.

PAST	**ISSUE**	FUTURE
Control	Information	Meaning
Creativity	Innovation	Execution
Resources	Efficiency	Resourcefulness
Manage	Change	Lead
Conditions	Engagement	Purpose

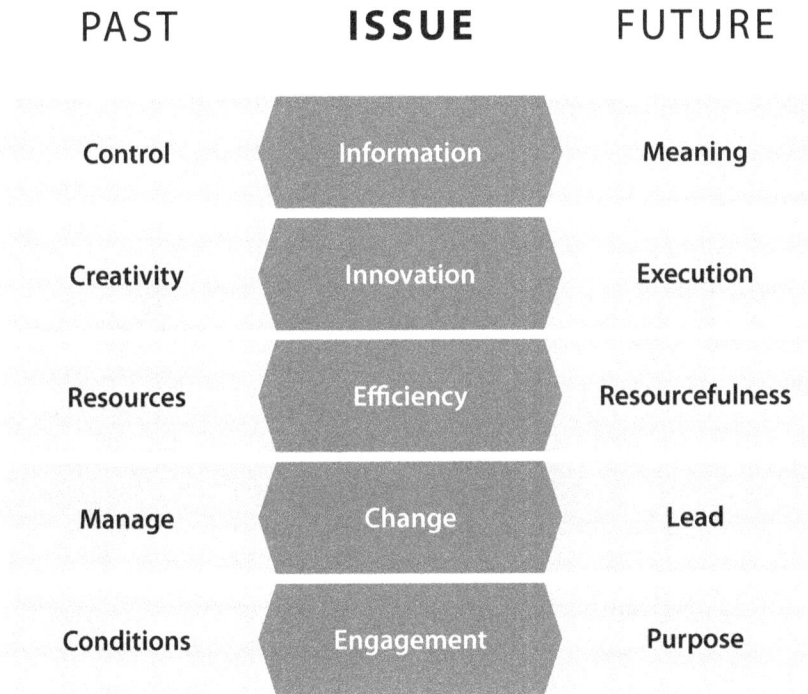

Figure 4. Five business issues focus

Make embracing change a culture not a project

As evidenced again and again throughout history and business, both ancient and recent, it's incredibly hard to change a system when you're living within the system. For those operating in large, complex organisational structures with many moving parts, leading change and disruption is incredibly difficult.

Take this story from the advertising industry. A dominant advertising agency in New York found that smaller, more agile agencies were stealing market share, yet the company was unable to respond because of the size and inflexibility of their business. So what did they do instead? They created their own small and agile agency to take on the market, in direct competition with their own parent company. Separate offices, its own culture, and a clear direction; save us from ourselves.

As a leader, you must be positively paranoid and look for where complacency has set in.

They created a culture which embraces competition. They embrace it so much they're happy to compete against themselves.

Make leadership the lever of change

Kelly Johnson, chief research engineer for Lockheed and Martin, the American aerospace and technology company, formed 'Skunk Works' in response to the need to evolve and expand projects in a company already at capacity.[2] There was so little space in the factory that Johnson hired an old circus tent and moved his people out there. Skunk Works was essentially a small independent team ruled by a series of Kelly Johnson principles: The project manager had complete control of each project, the number of people involved was severely restricted, a minimum number of reports were submitted (though those that were must be thorough), and elite engineers were given hands-on access and freedom with the project. Johnson believed that a flexible and nimble team was necessary to drive creativity and change. His team was responsible for creating many groundbreaking engineering feats in record breaking time, including the Blackbird, arguably the best jet plane ever built.

As a leader, you must be positively paranoid and look for where complacency has set in. Go about training focus and energy on the inertia of the old. If nothing changes on your watch, you are a manager, not a leader.

Summary

To be a great changemonger, you need to step outside the machine of your own success and disrupt yourself. It's about having an appetite for change and a renegade mindset that enables you to thrive in disruption and swim upstream. And if you do? Like Amazon Cloud, you will be able to offer your clients what they actually want better than anyone else. Like the advertising company, you will be able to operate with flexibility outside of business structures. Like Kelly Johnson, you will have the ability to lead confidently in a crowded workplace. That's what being an internal thought leader is all about.

ONLINE REFERENCES

1. Cade Metz. 2015. *Dell. EMC. HP. Cisco. These Tech Giants are the Walking Dead.* https://www.wired.com/2015/10/meet-walking-dead-hp-cisco-dell-emc-ibm-oracle/

2. Peter Garrison. 2010. *Head Skunk.* http://www.airspacemag.com/history-of-flight/head-skunk-5960121/

DISCUSSION IDEAS

1 Identify three ways your business
could profit from change.

_____

_____

_____

2 What are our 'sacred cows', those things
we hold holy in the business?

_____

_____

_____

3 How are we playing it safe?

_____

_____

_____

4 What is our status quo? What would
waging war on that look like?

_____

_____

_____

5 Discuss the culture present in your business and imagine a 'skunk works. What would this team do differently?

_____

_____

_____

6 Exploring the five big ideas in the model, can you come up with two more that exist in your business and do the before and after contrast frame on them?

_____

_____

_____

4

THE FUTURE OF WORK

What will the future of work be? Will we go to an office or work from home? Will we work as employees or will we all become contractors? If robots take 50% of the jobs that currently exist without replacing them with new ones, what then? This chapter explores some of these themes and should get a juicy conversation going about the future of work.

F or as long as I can remember, the G7 nations have ruled the world. Now, apart from Germany, each is in debt akin to teenagers with credit cards. The macro economic conversation should not really be simplified to that extent, but one thing is clear: the nations that have ruled for the last 50 years won't still be ruling by the end of this decade, let alone for the next 50 years. This means that the workforce habits and ways of working in these countries are going to need to adapt or risk becoming extinct.

Your best and brightest don't want to work in factories anymore.

By 2020 the G7 economies will be overtaken by Brazil, Russia, India, and China. In the first quarter of 2015, China surpassed the USA in Gross Domestic Product, the mere suggestion of which would have been laughed at only a few decades ago.

Richard Florida, in his book *The Rise of the Creative Class*, makes a case for the modern knowledge worker being in search of meaning, their driving force being the pursuit of happiness. Or more accurately, the journey to self-actualisation.

> Self-actualisation is popularly associated with Abraham Maslow, who argued that people's motivations are dominated at first by the fulfilment of basic survival needs. As these basic needs are fulfilled the dominating motivation becomes love and esteem. Further along, a person naturally gravitates to figuring out and realising one's fullest potential, or self-actualisation. Later, Maslow himself would critique this theory and add that self-actualisation happens when one surrenders to a higher goal external to the self, through altruism and spirituality.

Dan Pink, in his book *A Whole New Mind*, makes the same case as Florida and Maslow but through a different lens, focusing on personal and professional success. He notes that as people easily attain basic needs, there is a shift in pursuing meaning in life — spiritually and professionally. Pink says there are common characteristics among those that get ahead professionally and those who are fulfilled personally, and these involve inventiveness, empathy, and meaning.

If you read either of these works side by side with something on outsourcing, you begin to see the possibilities for a new world of work. A world where we leverage talent by being open and flexible as employers and leaders. Your best and brightest don't want to work in factories anymore. They are more like DaVinci and less like Henry Ford.

The war for talent is not a war

At the big end of town, it's the same dynamic just playing out in a slow awakening. For the last decade we have been bandying about the term 'the war for talent'. Many say, tongue in cheek, that the war for talent is over — talent won. But that is not true.

While we have been playing the engagement game in an attempt to get more out of the workers, we are missing the big idea; talented people want to be inspired. That's probably not going to happen in your 8–6 workspace. Make it as funky as you like, but really all you are doing is making the factory more pleasant. Your great minds, the thought leaders in your business, are desperate to break out and get inspired offline and on, but they're doing so on their terms. They love the cafe for its white noise and lack of interruption by managers. They want to do great work, deep thinking work, they want to come up with ideas and have the space and mandate to implement them. But are you letting them?

Make it as funky as you like but really all you are doing is making the factory more pleasant.

It is not all roses and lollipops for the talent, many highly qualified talented people are out of work, some trained for roles that no longer exist. In a 2014 national survey conducted by Graduate Careers Australia for universities, it was found that thirty two per cent of university graduates were still unemployed four months after graduation.[1] The analysis points to the oversupply of graduates as the main reason. At the same time some, roles that people trained for no longer exist, and companies are using less people to fulfil the roles that remain.

Then finish off the perfect storm with robots. This decade is going to see not only the impact of offshoring as the world gets flatter, but also the increasingly intelligent automating of many workflows we currently require talented staff to operate.

This is the challenge for workers in the next decade: how to remain competitive in the new world of outsourcing and offshoring. If they don't there won't be work. Contrast the critical path for both offshore and onshore workers (see Figure 5 on page 41).

Our ways of working need to adapt or risk becoming extinct.

We need to evolve our focus and move from the factory model to the Hollywood model. It's about engaging talent in projects that inspire them. And setting them up to do this in creative ways. The 9–5 work schedule died last decade, it went to the same place as 'work-life balance'; the land of myths and unicorns. We the talented are happy to work our butts off, if we believe our work matters, our cultures are worth belonging to, and our leaders are worth following.(see Figure 6 on page 42)

This model explores the idea of how Hollywood engages talent. Hollywood brings amazing individuals together on massive projects, focusing on bringing the best talent possible to collaborate on 100 million dollar companies that form, profit, and sometimes flop at the box office. Hollywood drives intense collaborative projects with a combined commercial and artistic focus. In the Hollywood model, you as a leader are more like a director than a manager.

	OFFSHORE	ONSHORE
NOW	Cheap labour that talks with a funny accent	Expensive labour with a sense of entitlement
SOON	Cheap, enthusiastic and highly proficient labour	Expensive labour that is out of work
NEXT	Great value, service professionals with an extraordinary work ethic	Overqualified labour that cannot compete globally

Figure 5. Offshore versus onshore

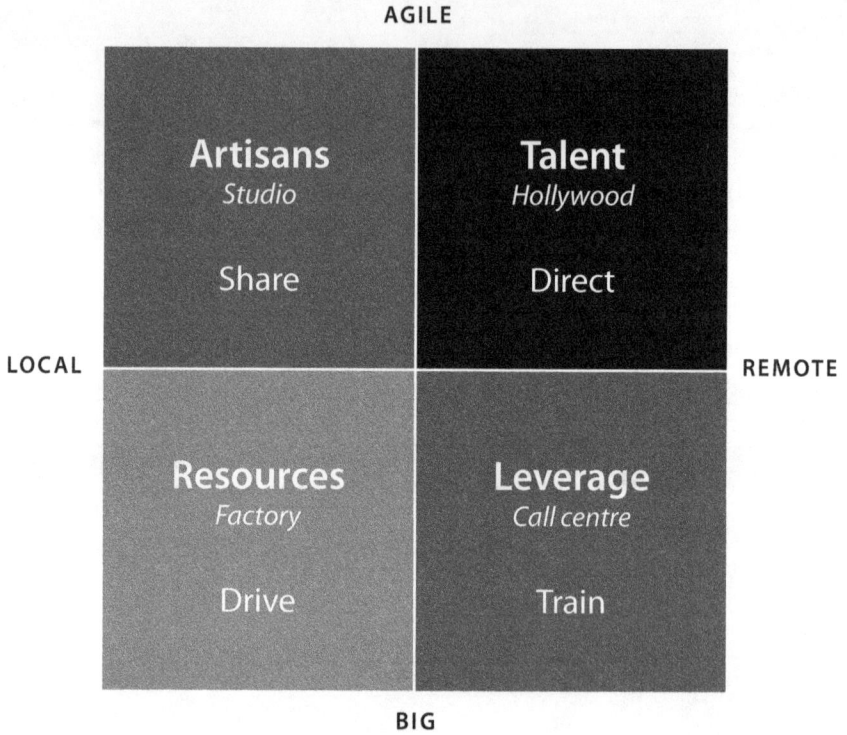

AGILE

LOCAL

Artisans	Talent
Studio	*Hollywood*
Share	Direct

Resources	Leverage
Factory	*Call centre*
Drive	Train

REMOTE

BIG

Figure 6. The four business cultural styles

When the Hollywood model is not available, Artisans will come together in a communal studio vibe, occasionally collaborating on projects but mostly sharing resources. The small studio mindset is often a small game version of Hollywood, resisting the 'man' staying out of the 'machine' and as a result, there is often an angst-ridden struggle as the artisans in the studio create real art. Often the studio can't scale or leverage talent effectively.

Contrast this with the idea of running a factory. Humans are not the 'talent', they are 'resources' that you drive to get things done.

Compare the Hollywood model to the Call centre model. Here you are leveraging lowest common denominator and creating consistency through training.

This year The Grid, an artificially intelligent website design platform, will come online seeking to make expensive graphic designers, and their appreciation of hue, style guides and placement, unnecessary. [2] Whether The Grid pops as an idea or not, it's the heralding of in-your-face AI. Florida said these highly skilled aestheticians, the talented designers, would become the new talented workforce. He is right. When it counts, it will really matter. Yet it doesn't count in as many situations as they might hope and as a result, they too are under threat.

Our prediction is that the new workforce will need to have an entrepreneurial spirit regardless of whether they are employed or running their own businesses.

Architects are extremely valuable and many in the developed world use an architect to design the dream house on the perfect plot of land. Soon though the rise of global architect design platforms will enable you to kind of design like an architect. The options will be extraordinary and many elements of the build will be prefabricated, turning skilled builders into allen-key-IKEA house assemblers. There will be less loss of aesthetic than you might think.

1. REPAIR
annoying systems attacked
Lose the rules

2. INSTALL
tech improves workflows
Don't do boring

3. SHARE
Demand for better up
Make great stuff

4. NEXT
whole new world
Old ways are dead

Figure 7.   The typical cycle of disruption

A simple iPhone-like device will be placed on the site and it will read the weather, wind and sun spots and create the perfectly oriented property design. A series of Skype-like conversations with your architectural concierge will enable better personalisation in a way that is convenient and efficient.

The cycle of disruption goes like this:

- Damaged and annoying systems get attacked and ultimately replaced

- Simple processes and workflows get replaced by technology

- Consumers demand a higher level of sophistication and service

- Finally, the old ways of doing things go through a fundamental change and no longer work

Businesses and their leaders therefore need to:

- Question existing business models (positive paranoia)

- Increase their novel insights (fresh perspectives)

- Become sense makers (command context)

- Obsess about customers (intimacy and inspiration)

- Build cultures worth belonging to (performance environments)

My prediction—and I am not alone in this—is that the new workforce will need to have an entrepreneurial spirit regardless of whether they are employed or running their own businesses. The new workforce will need the ability to read the value chain and make a contribution that is a game changer. They need to be able to deploy products and services into the marketplace with a scientist's zeal, running experiment after experiment, OK with failure as simply a form of feedback. They will need to become creators, not just innovators. They will need to adapt. They will need a bias towards action, towards making things happen and being extraordinary executors.

If you work for someone you need to:

- Work as if you own it

- Create value where none existed previously

- Launch ideas experimentally

- Pivot and adapt rapidly

- Implement ruthlessly

In a nutshell, future workers will need to shift from entitled to entrepreneurial. From acting like employees in factories who can turn up and clock on, forgetting about work at the end of the day, to instead carry the responsibility that their new creative role demands. Creatives never stop thinking, they know that the muse comes at the strangest times, not 9–5. The future of work is bright as long as you are not dull.

ONLINE REFERENCES

1. Graduate Careers Australia, GCA, 2014. *Grad Employment and Salary Outcomes of Recent Higher Education Graduates Stats.* [Online]. 1, 1-10. Available at: http://www.graduatecareers.com.au/wp-content/uploads/2014/12/GCA_GradStats_2014.pdf

2. The Grid. https://thegrid.io/

BOOKS MENTIONED

Florida, R., 2002. *The Rise of the Creative Class.* 1st ed. United States: Basic Books.

Pink, D., 2006. *A Whole New Mind: Why Right-Brainers Will Rule the Future.* 1st ed. United States: Riverhead Books.

DISCUSSION IDEAS

1 What do you think of the phrase 'war for talent'?

_____
_____
_____

2 How do you feel about offshore workers?

_____
_____
_____

3 Which countries do you imagine will be ruling the economy in 10 years time?

_____
_____
_____

4 Looking at the offshore onshore model, what are you thinking, feeling or knowing?

_____
_____
_____

5 Reviewing the cycle of disruption, are there any case studies you can think of where this has applied?

_____

_____

_____

6 Do we have any damaged or annoying systems worth examining?

_____

_____

_____

7 Have you heard of the term intrapreneur?

_____

_____

_____

8 Does your business encourage this idea? If so where and if not why?

_____

_____

_____

9 The idea of projects not roles is interesting, do you have anything to share around that?

_____

_____

_____

PRESSURE MAKES DIAMONDS

The world is experiencing change at an exponentially increasing rate. It's creating situations where leaders in every industry and every environment are under increasing pressure to perform. Pressure clearly affects our ability to work effectively. But it would be a mistake to think that pressure only affects us in a negative way. In fact, pressure is key to maximising the performance of some of the world's greatest leaders.

How do you respond to pressure? Does it make you or break you?

In his book *Antifragile*, Nassim Nicholas Taleb makes the point that some things are better when they are treated roughly, the opposite of handle with care. He unpacks quite convincingly that we need pressure and stress.

World class performers in any field have already responded to the pressure of their environment and expectations by stepping things up. They have developed their capacity to tolerate stress and have turned that pressure into drive. This is the road less travelled.

Most people reach a degree of personal comfort and don't stretch the edges of what's possible. They reject the pressure. They decide that this is as fit as they will be, or that's the hours they will work, that's the way they will work and they don't change things up or take things to the next level. They plateau. They listen to music from when they were young and sexy and simply don't move on. It's more comfortable that way.

Essentially, they're settling where they are to avoid pressure, rather than seeing the pressure as a necessary part of the journey to self-actualisation.

What are our needs, and how are we motivated to fulfil them? Maslow (1943) stated that people are motivated to achieve certain needs, and that some needs take precedence over others. Our most basic need is for physical survival, and this will be the first thing that motivates our behaviour. Once that level is fulfilled we become motivated by the next level up, and so on.

Maslow

Looking through Maslow's hierarchy of needs (see Figure 8 on page 53), we can see our needs have changed. Eighty years ago the most pressing need was to fulfil basic survival drives. Our responses to pressure were built around fulfilling our biological and physiological needs, and our safety needs. We needed to make sure we

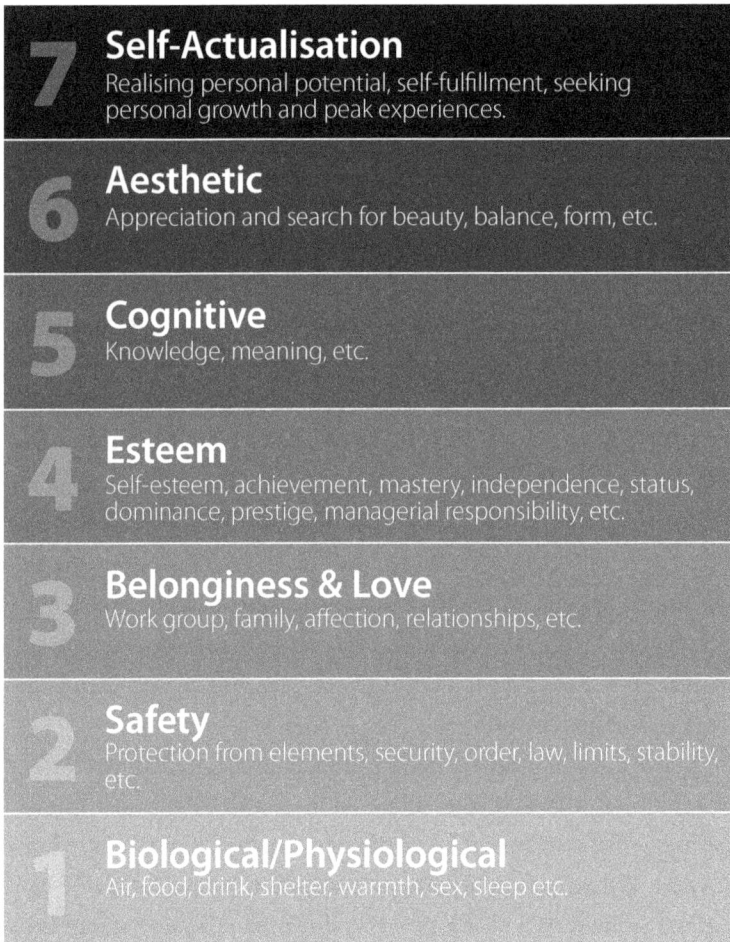

7 Self-Actualisation
Realising personal potential, self-fulfillment, seeking personal growth and peak experiences.

6 Aesthetic
Appreciation and search for beauty, balance, form, etc.

5 Cognitive
Knowledge, meaning, etc.

4 Esteem
Self-esteem, achievement, mastery, independence, status, dominance, prestige, managerial responsibility, etc.

3 Belonginess & Love
Work group, family, affection, relationships, etc.

2 Safety
Protection from elements, security, order, law, limits, stability, etc.

1 Biological/Physiological
Air, food, drink, shelter, warmth, sex, sleep etc.

Figure 8. Abraham Maslow's Hierarchy of Needs

had somewhere dry and safe to live. We needed to make sure we had enough food and water. Now, in the culture we live in, we have almost unlimited access to food, resources, and shelter. These needs have been fulfilled. Obviously, we still need to eat and sleep and look after our safety, but the pressure upon us to do these things is light, and easily relieved.

World class performers have developed their capacity to tolerate stress and have turned that pressure into drive.

Maslow noted only one in a hundred people become fully self-actualised, because our society rewards motivation primarily based on esteem, love and other social needs.

We need to recognise that the pressure we feel in our day to day lives is simply an expression of an internal drive to fulfil the next level of needs. Once we make this decision, we're able to see the pressure as a cue to solve or achieve a missing need. This is a much more appropriate response to pressure! Pressure is an incentive to do things, to go and solve a problem. Realise that, and get to work!

Life is a series of moments, or inflection points. Moments when you get to decide what you will do with a curve ball or how you will choose to respond to a given set of circumstances. Cavett Robert, the founder of the National Speakers Association, famously said "Life is a grind stone, whether it wears you down or polishes you up is up to you."

Top performers grow their capacity to handle pressure, under performers simply don't. In Carol Dweck's book *Mindset* she unpacks the fixed versus growth mindset (see Figure 9 on page 55).

A fixed mindset means a belief that intelligence (or any other cognitive capability) is set at birth. A growth mindset implies a belief that these things can change if given attention and effort. Focus on a child's results, good or bad, and the kid forms fixed opinions about

FIXED MINDSET	GROWTH MINDSET
Avoid challenges	Embrace challenges
Give up easily due to obstacles	Persist despite obstacles
See effort as fruitless	See effort as path to mastery
Ignore useful feedback	Learn from criticism
Be threatened by others' success	Be inspired by others' success

Acknowledgement: Carol Dweck

Figure 9. Dweck's fixed versus growth mindset

whether they are any good at something. Focus on the effort the kid put in and you have the chance to develop a kid who will have a go at anything.

While we don't specifically aim to manage the emotions of everyone in the Thought Leaders Business School program — that's the job of great programs such as Landmark — we do recognise the frames of reference people experience when put under the pump. The better that thought leaders are able to process their own pressure, the better their lives and practices will be (see Figure 10 on page 57).

The vertical axis, Affirmation–Transformation, represents intent. If you're below the line you're seeking reassurance. If you're above the line you're seeking to make improvements.

The horizontal axis, Inspiration–Implementation, covers the spectrum from consuming to creating. If you're on the left side then you're seeking ideas. If you're on the right you're seeking progress. The left is think, right is do.

Everybody lives in every quadrant of the model at various points in their life. But for those of us seeking more from ourselves, our goal should always be to move up, and to the right.

If you want to thrive in the disrupted future, it might be time to explore putting yourself under the pump.

The better that leaders are able to process their own pressure, the better their lives will be.

At Thought Leaders Business School, we're always helping the tribe move above the line and to the right, so that they get into action. We didn't set out to design a personal development course, though a great deal of personal development happens in parallel when you seek extraordinary results.

So how do we actually move around the model? When you are under the pump your pressure responses kick in. The two primary ways we respond to pressure is to seek affirmation or transformation.

TRANSFORMATION

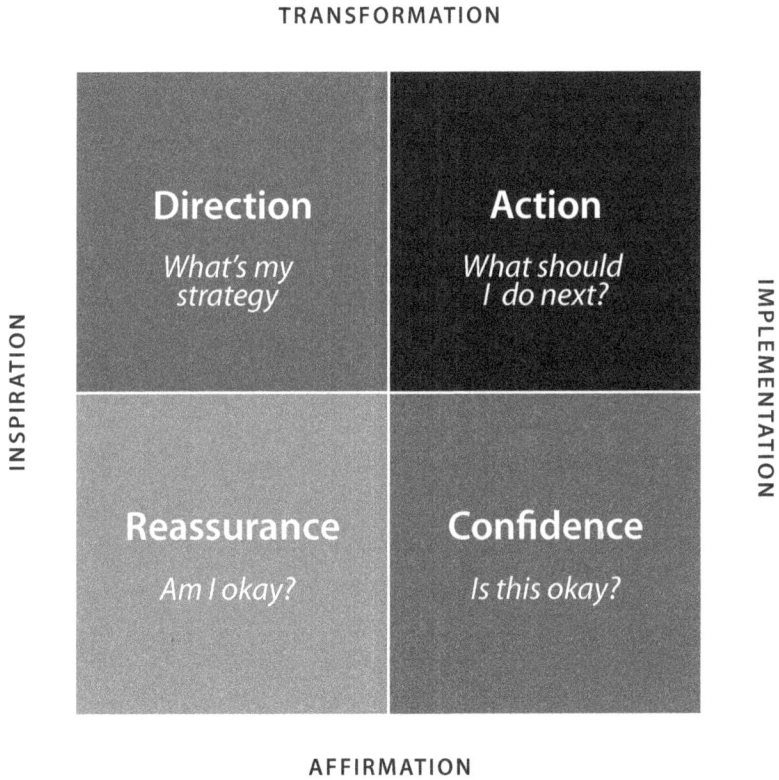

	Direction *What's my strategy*	Action *What should I do next?*	
INSPIRATION	Reassurance *Am I okay?*	Confidence *Is this okay?*	IMPLEMENTATION

AFFIRMATION

Figure 10. Transformation versus affirmation

Those seeking affirmation will ask "Am I ok?" "Is this ok?" Those seeking transformation will either ideate or create. Whether seeking affirmation or transformation, everybody can choose to think or choose to do.

Pressure is an incentive to do things, to go and solve a problem. Realise that, and get to work!

In her great book *The Nine Things Successful People Do Differently*, Dr Heidi Grant Halvorson unpacks a process for shifting your behaviours.

Not everyone will put themselves under extra pressure intentionally and maybe it's not for everyone. However, if you want to thrive in the disrupted future, it might be time to explore putting yourself under the pump. Pressure is not the only path to greatness, but it's a solid workout. Do you go to the gym and bemoan the presence of the treadmill, because it causes you pain? No! You understand that subjecting your body to that particular trial will make it stronger, you make a decision, and get into action.

If you want to thrive in the disrupted future, it might be time to explore putting yourself under the pump.

ONLINE REFERENCES

99U. (2014). *Heidi Grant Halvorson: The Incredible Benefits of a "Get Better" Mindset.* [Online Video]. 13 February 2014. Available from: https://vimeo.com/86610705.

Trevor Ragan. (2014). *Carol Dweck — A Study on Praise and Mindsets.* [Online Video]. 30 January 2014. Available from: https://www.youtube.com/watch?v=NWv1VdDeoRY.

BOOKS MENTIONED

Dweck, Ph.D, C., 2016. *Mindset: The New Psychology of Success.* 2nd ed. United States: Random House.

Grant Halvorson Ph.D, H., 2012. *Nine Things Successful People Do Differently.* 1st ed. United States: Harvard Business Review Press.

Taleb, N., 2012. *Antifragile: Things That Gain from Disorder.* 1st ed. United States: Random House.

DISCUSSION IDEAS

1 What things in our business are antifragile and get better when treated without care?

_____
_____
_____

2 Where in your life have you levelled up so that what was previously pressure is now normalised?

_____
_____
_____

3 What kind of music do you listen to?

_____
_____
_____

4 Study the Maslow's Hierarchy of Needs model and share what you think about when you look at it.

_____
_____
_____

5 What are the pressure points you are experiencing in your role at the moment?

_____

_____

_____

6 Reviewing the list of fixed versus growth mindset distinctions, which side of the model do you find yourself on?

_____

_____

_____

7 Looking at the transformation model and the line that separates the bottom two quadrants and the top, whats coming up for you?

_____

_____

_____

8 Where do you reckon you could take on more pressure?

_____

_____

_____

9 Discuss this with reference to personal and professional domains.

_____

_____

_____

THE PROGRESS PARADOX

There is a tension between being comfortable and pushing yourself. If you practice mindfulness and are ambitious you may find yourself at philosophical odds from time to time. Work life balance and performance deadlines seem at odds. Praising effort over results seems challenging when numbers matter in business. A lot of this tension sits in the space explored in this chapter.

I n 1903 George Bernard Shaw wrote a piece of work titled *Maxims for Revolutionists*

A famous quote from it sets up this chapter:

> "The reasonable man adapts himself to the world; the unreasonable one persists in trying to adapt the world to himself. Therefore all progress depends on the unreasonable man."

I have worked in transformation coaching, mentoring and learning environments for enough years now to see a real paradox between progress and fulfilment. Brian Tracy names it well in his book *Focal Point* when he explains that those who get things done have a sense of urgency around what they do. They are blessed with dissatisfaction.

That being said Goethe the 17th-century German philosopher said:

> "Seldom should we let the urgent take the place of the important but oftentimes we do."

This very quote prompted the late Dr Stephen Covey to pen his landmark book *First Things First*, a must read for those interested in getting stuff done. It's this tension between creating a sense of urgency like a false deadline and focusing on what really matters that I'd like to explore in this chapter.

If you link achievement to happiness you are likely to be filling holes the rest of your life.

The paradox is that we often try to achieve things as a way of being happy or being fulfilled. I reckon this is fraught with error. If you link achievement to happiness you are likely to be filling holes the rest of your life and, no matter what success you achieve, you will never be satisfied or fulfilled. One symptom of this is the person who identifies their sense of worth and self through what they have done.

Dangerous rocky reefs for sure. I think that Oliver Burkeman's book *The Antidote* covers this off brilliantly, especially chapter four where he exposes the dogma of goal setting as negative to success.

For those into surfing, my friend Layne Beachley's biography *Beneath the Waves* is a real-life practical example of this. Seven-time world champion surfer she explains how the first six titles were filling holes, proving she was worthy. The seventh title was so much more powerful because it came from love not lack. Brilliantly inspiring story!

The sign of an evolved mind is the ability to handle contradiction, paradox, and ambiguity.

I think that the key to success is disassociating progress and happiness, as well as being driven by the desire to create in a pure form (see Figure 11 on page 66). Not to be complete or appreciated or respected, but just to BE a creator. This is the key to progress and happiness. It's a bit like the Zen Buddhist Koans, such as holding on tight with an open palm. The paradox is the point to focus on. It holds the answer and the prescription without the heavy directive of dogma.

Drive and progress fight each other all the time; the fix is to be a creator not just a doer, tinkerer, or simply someone who is always gunna do something different with their life.

People who get things done create a tension between what they have and what they want, as well as where they are and where they want to be.

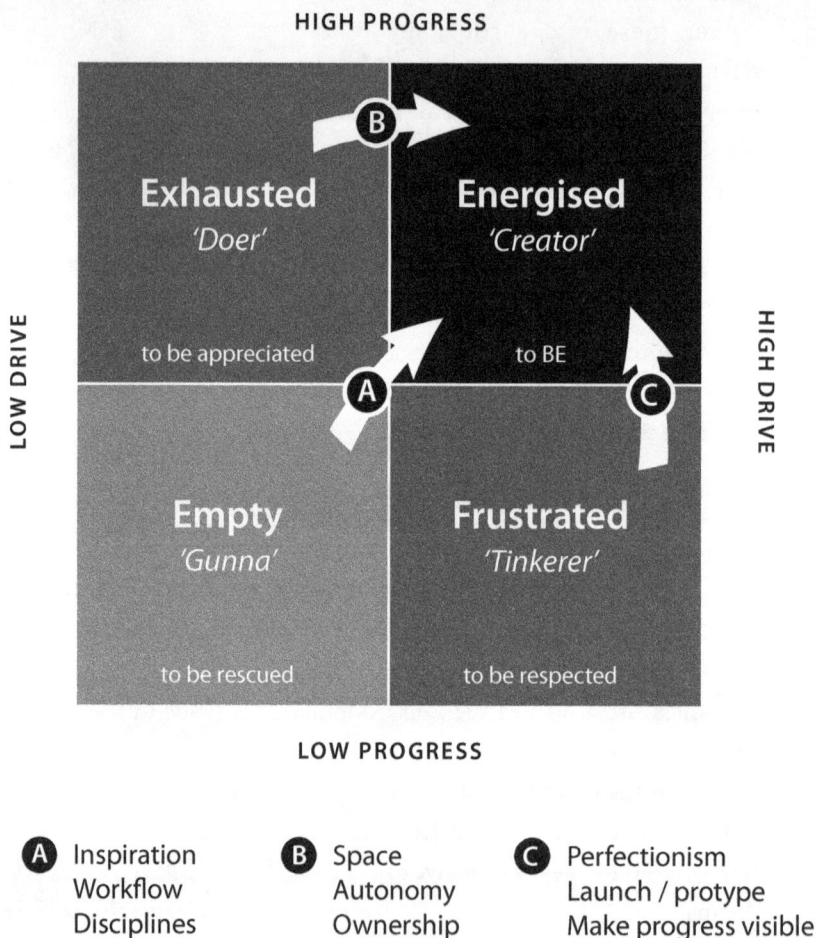

Figure 11.   Being a creator is key to managing
the progress paradox.

Empty promises

If you find your self stuck in the bottom left of this quadrant you will feel like the reason you do things is to fill some hole in your belief. You feel broken, less somehow, not good enough. This drive to be complete is not mindful; it's an empty promise, a forever moving goal post. Develop disciplines, get a workflow that works for you, and seek inspiration.

Exhausted doers

If you get things done but feel under appreciated, then you might need to create some space, do things by yourself and for yourself. Enough with the sacrifice and self-sacrifice. It's a bit like buying love, you do the work and then look for the appreciation. Ironically the more you look for it, the more you will get taken for granted. Create for creativity's sake, to do something good, to birth an idea or nudge the needle. Don't do so that others can say 'wow you are amazing.' You will just end up on the treadmill of disappointment.

Frustrated tinkerers

For a 'tinkerer' nothing is ever finished. They want to create great work and are their own worst critic. They suffer from perfectionism and need to get OK with ideas like; MVP (minimum viable product), prototyping, and launching before they are ready. Play games around making progress visible, look for little ways to game the system, simple milestones that help you stay in momentum.

I once had a visiting martial arts teacher who, when asked about his disobedience of a fairly strict dogma in the school, said that the sign of an evolved mind is the ability to handle contradiction, paradox and ambiguity. This is the key to fulfilment and progress being reconciled. It's about getting comfortable in the space between two ideas.

Be happy no matter what, find happiness in simple things and beware of the drive to achieve as a means to an end. This then stretches into topics like suffocation and *Affluenza,* a book by Clive Hamilton, which makes the point (a little bit socialist in bent) that more stuff is not the key to happiness. I get it. It reaches into topics of mindfulness and contentment. As Louise Hay says in her book *You Can Heal Your Life*

> "We are not happy because we do or have, we have and do because we are happy."

BUT… that does not mean do nothing. The third choice that breaks the paradox is to make things happen like an artist does. Your art can come in many forms; it doesn't have to be marble and paint.

Da Vinci famously said

> "I have been impressed with the urgency of doing. Knowing is not enough; we must apply. Being willing is not enough; we must do."

People who get things done create a tension between what they have and what they want, as well as where they are and where they want to be. This tension, and the subsequent need to progress things, is for me the meaning of life if done right. Create!

So, it is appropriately circular that we come back to another of Shaw's quotes

> "Life isn't about finding yourself. Life is about creating yourself."

3 Actions

1. **Become productivity obsessed.** Find out how to achieve more in a day than most do in a week. Stretch and grow your capacity to work. Overcome frictions, remove procrastinations, and each day try to create something.

2. **Surrender instantly.** The minute you do create something, let go. Learn the art of surrender, disassociate from the act of creation. You are not what you do or have.

3. **Be allergic to mediocrity.** Ask more of yourself and others than is reasonable.

BOOKS MENTIONED

Burkeman, O., 2012. *The Antidote: Happiness for People Who Can't Stand Positive Thinking.* 1st ed. United States: Farrar, Straus and Giroux.

Covey, S., 1994. *First Things First.* 1st ed. United States: Simon & Schuster.

Gordon, M. with Layne Beachley, 2008. *Layne Beachley: Beneath The Waves.* 1st ed. United Kingdom: Ebury Press

Hamilton, C., 2006. *Affluenza: When Too Much is Never Enough.* 1st ed. Australia: Allen & Unwin.

Hay, L., 1994. *You Can Heal Your Life.* 1st ed. United States: Hay House Inc.

Shaw, G., 2013. *Maxims for Revolutionists.* 1st ed. United States: CreateSpace Independent Publishing Platform

Tracy, B., 2002. *Focal Point: A Proven System to Simplify Your Life, Double Your Productivity, and Achieve All Your Goals.* 1st ed. United States: AMACOM.

DISCUSSION IDEAS

1 Have you ever lost yourself in an act of creation and lost all sense of time?

_____

_____

_____

2 Review the Important versus urgent model in Coveys book *First Things First*. Now, list out some quadrant two activities you could work on.

_____

_____

_____

3 Where in your life could you create a greater sense of urgency?

_____

_____

_____

4 Have a discussion with the people around you around the idea 'You are not your work'.

_____

_____

_____

5   Have a discussion about the four quadrants in Figure 11

_____

_____

_____

THE GENIE
IN THE BOTTLE

Success creates its own problems. Most industry or market disruptors come from out of the blue. Not because they are smarter than the incumbent industry leaders, but probably because of a baked-in success superstition that prevents adaptation. This chapter is about exploring how to get out of your own way on the journey to the future and to consider how you may have a stability bias that is preventing you becoming all you can be as an individual, team or business.

F uturists spend more time analysing the forces that drive change than they do trying to predict the actual changes likely to occur. It makes sense that outsiders cannot predict the path of an industry market, technology, or culture with any real accuracy. Instead, it is more logical that the people who are within a certain 'space' are the ones to make the choices that shape the future of that space. Innovative builders should shape the future of construction, innovative lawyers should shape the future of governance, and innovative technologists should shape the future of gadgets. Alan Kay, the creator of Graphical User Interface, said it well when he suggested "The only way to predict the future is to create it." That's a nice bit of rah rah right there.

It's hard to read the label when you are the genie in the bottle.

There is only one problem with this 'self-directing future' theory, and that is that rarely does history show industry leaders as the ones to lead change. They are often bound by their success; it's as if they have decided that their biography is their destiny. It really is hard to read the label when you are the genie in the bottle.

Kodak invented the technology that put them out of business (well almost); they were in the business of better photos, and we wanted to share memories. Nokia failed to see the shift that the iPhone created and in under a year lost catastrophic market share. The rich industrialists of North America who laid the railway tracks and opened a nation failed to get into aviation early enough; they were in the steel and railway business and failed to seize the transport opportunity.

In each case, smart, intelligent industry leaders did not see the writing on the wall and failed to adapt. Not because they were clueless; indeed their very success was built on a series of strong foundations. Foundations that kept them grounded in the 'success habits' that made them successful. They didn't fail to adapt because they were stupid, they failed to adapt because they were wildly successful. The problem with foundations is that they are useless in a zero gravity environment. It is counterintuitive to let go of your gravity anchors, your identity anchors, and your success anchors. Success breeds stability; it's the point of success. This stability though becomes a liability in an age of extraordinary change.

Letting the genie out of the bottle

It takes a certain courage to put the status quo on notice, to disrupt yourself. And yet that's what we all need to do if we are going to lead our families, businesses, and industries into this decade of disruption.

In his book *The Age of Paradox* Charles Handy unpacks the sigmoid growth curve as this ever-present S-shaped curve that plots not only the life of any organism or the life-cycle of any product, but also the life of an organisation, the progress of civilisation, and even the course of a relationship. Handy stated, "The world keeps changing. It is one of the paradoxes of success that the things and the ways which got you where you are, are seldom those that keep you there."

The key to sustained success is recognising not only that it's essential to reinvent, but to begin doing so before the idea/culture/people/etc, responsible for your current success inevitably begins to decline. To start a new curve, right at the moment when all the usual indicators might suggest sticking to the current course.

History rarely shows industry leaders as the ones to lead change.

The first observation is to understand that there is a dip before there is a period of growth. This is the moment after a decision when the decision is truly tested. Stefan Kerwell, a published authority on the S curve, relates this to the time when a new born baby loses

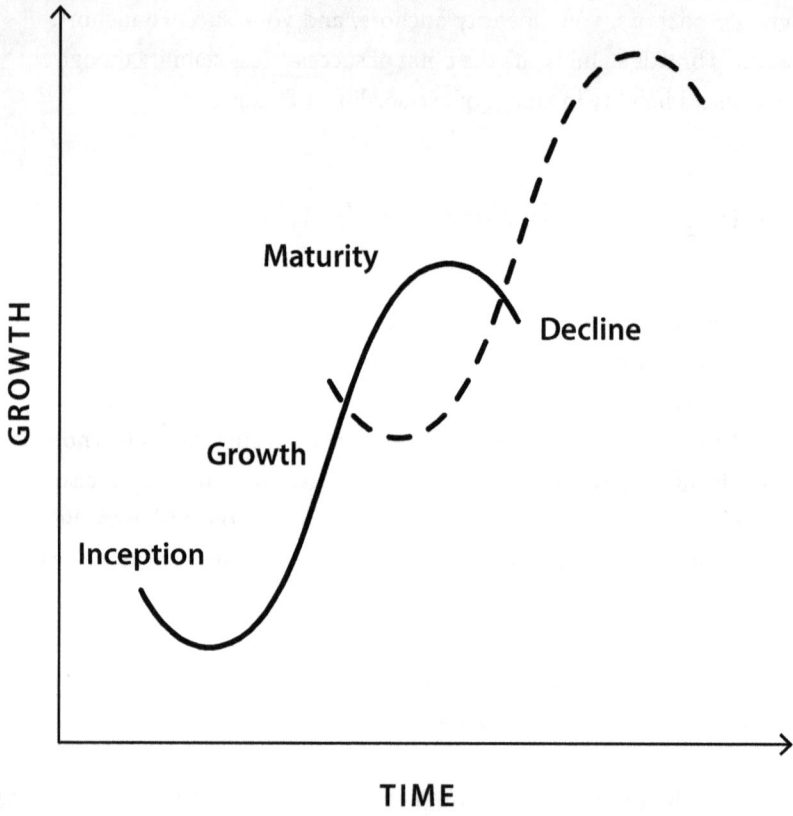

Figure 12.   Sigmoid growth curve

weight for a while. First-time parents panic if they are not aware that this is normal. Think of it more as the squat before you jump.

The second thing to notice about S curve theory is that two curves co-exist for a while. This time is often called 'the period of great confusion'. It's into this space that duelling ideas may need to co-exist for a while. This is a time of contradiction, ambiguity and paradox. It's a time when a quarantined 'skunkworks' might serve a business, or it's the time when a leader needs to protect and run interference for a team that needs to operate outside of the existing cultural rules. One line of action needs to continue its upward growth while the other will be struggling to find its feet. Both need to be supported.

> *They didn't fail to adapt because they were stupid, they failed to adapt because they were wildly successful.*

The third observation to make is around the increased speed of change that this next decade will hold. The curve is compressing. Changes will happen more often. So the ability to be agiler, to be more willing to fail and to be open to new, counterintuitive processes is a competitive advantage.

Positive paranoia

So how do we know when to start a new change? Just because you are paranoid doesn't mean you are not being followed! This idea that positive paranoia is a strength in the now and the future is key to making sure you are not the genie 'stuck' in the bottle. Positive paranoia is the core idea behind doomsday thinking and scenario planning.

There is a benefit to being a little paranoid, spending time asking yourself the questions that cause a fear of loss, a clench in your belly. These include questions like: What if the truth I adhere to is false? If our primary way of making money disappeared tomorrow, what would we do? What should we do if Amazon eats our server business?

These questions, or more accurately the issues they unravel, highlight blind spots for many leaders. This is why it's so hard to do. It's like looking a tiger in the eyes. Many won't allow this kind of conversation to enter their team meetings. It's as if by entertaining what might go wrong you're disloyal to 'confidence'. You may become labelled a negative thinker and called out as being counter culture. Do it anyway. Question everything, and prepare solutions for challenges that haven't happened yet.

Most companies wait too long. That change needs to begin before the first curve reaches its peak. This is when the team has the resources and the energy to start a new change. The difficulty is that there have not yet been any signs that this change is necessary! Attempts to bring in change are often met by resistance, so it's tempting to put it off.

Charles Roxburgh, a director at McKinsey and Co, explains the power of scenario thinking:

> "Scenarios allow people to challenge conventional wisdom. In large corporations, there is typically a status quo bias. After all, large sums of money, and many senior executives' careers have been invested in the core assumptions underpinning the current strategy—which means that challenging these assumptions can be difficult."

He goes on to explain the three major benefits to working alternate scenarios:

1. Scenarios uncover inevitable or near-inevitable futures

2. Scenarios protect against 'group think.'

3. Scenarios allow people to challenge conventional wisdom

We are often afraid to participate in 'what if?' conversations, we feel at some level that they erode confidence, seed uncertainty and prevent momentum. This is why it's hard to do; confidence becomes a camouflage that hides the tiger of change. Until one day it pounces on you as if by surprise. It's okay to question the path we are on; it's helpful to entertain dangerous ideas. This is why a business should encourage sceptics; this is why leaders need to surround themselves with 'no' people, those people willing to push back, fight for a position, even if—perhaps especially if—it's unpopular. In his book *Creativity, Inc* Ed Catmul discusses how at Pixar the culture of creative tension (healthy debate and disagreement) was critical to their continuous innovations and commercially creative success. His three tips for increasing the innovation include regularly sharing unfinished work, breaking down silos and empowering teams to do great work while at the same time embracing constraints.

This concept of dissent being constructive is picked up in the work of Harvard professor Linda Hill in her TED talk around generating collective creativity. Pixar was one of many global businesses she and her colleagues researched for creative, collaborative best practice. They identified that three things need to be in place to explore great creative collaborations: creative abrasion, creative agility and creative resolution.

Question everything, and prepare solutions for challenges that haven't happened yet.

Creative abrasion is about generating a market place of ideas through debate and trying to come up with a portfolio of alternatives. Creative agility is about being quick to pursue new ideas, experiment, fail and adjust. Creative resolution is about doing the decision making, so it has no compromise and no domination that you develop a patient and inclusive decision-making atmosphere.

These ideas are super cool, but hard to implement without a wholesale rebuild of your organisational culture and team's DNA.

Some little steps that help with setting the genie free: make status quo the enemy, cook your sacred cows, and stand for something.

Status quo is the state of normality, a plateau state which suggests that the chaos of change is over and we can catch our breath for a while. The time for plateaus is shrinking, and the idea that you can rest for a while should be rejected. Get on the front foot and be the disruptors. Lead the change.

It's okay to question the path we are on; it's helpful to entertain dangerous ideas.

Sacred cows are the metaphoric assumptions that are unquestionable. Make no doubt that outsiders have no compunction killing your sacred cows, after all, they make the best burgers! Challenge the assumptions, question everything. The more sacred the idea, the more threatened others are, the more dangerous and exposed to change you are, the better. Look for the most entrenched ideas and ask the dangerous, unpopular question. Do so from a positive paranoia based on being opportunistic, not afraid.

The third guiding light that helps genies get out of the bottle for a while is to stop fitting in, stop trying to please everyone. Pick a battle, throw a rock, take a stand. People and businesses become beige over time. The bigger you are, the more you become people pleasers. Your very scale means you become more conforming. So if you are big and complex and slow moving, then start to celebrate difference of opinion. The trick is to balance your confidence with politeness.

Stop fitting in and start standing out. Of course, doing this takes some understanding of nuance and subtlety. The energy of Jim Rohn's famous leadership statement captures the personality of this ethos so well:

"The challenge of leadership is to be strong, but not rude; be kind, but not weak; be bold, but not bully; be thoughtful, but not lazy; be humble, but not timid; be proud, but not arrogant; have humour but without folly."

ONLINE REFERENCES

McKinsey & Company. http://www.mckinsey.com/

TED. 2014. *TED Ideas Worth Spreading*. https://www.ted.com/talks/
linda_hill_how_to_manage_for_collective_creativity

BOOKS MENTIONED

Catmull, E., 2014. *Creativity, Inc.: Overcoming the Unseen Forces That Stand in the Way of True Inspiration*. 1st ed. United States: Random House.

Handy, C., 1994. *The Age of Paradox*. 1st ed. United States: Harvard Business School Press.

DISCUSSION IDEAS

1 How OK is your culture with tension,
debate and disagreement?

_____

_____

_____

2 Explore how to manage the generation and
implementation of ideas in your team.

_____

_____

_____

3 Where is 'status quo' in your business
or team holding you back?

_____

_____

_____

4 What actions can you take to fix that?

_____

_____

_____

5 What are your sacred cows?

_____
_____
_____

6 How would we do things differently
if they were not sacred?

_____
_____
_____

7 What do you stand for? What's your good fight? How
are you being a demand for this in the business?

_____
_____
_____

8

SKILLS IN THE FUTURE

This chapter is exploring the idea that what we used to know is maybe not that relevant in the not too distant future. It unpacks a series of skills and capabilities that futurists believe we need to arm ourselves with if we want to be ready for what comes next. The list makes sense, and yet when we look at corporate training or even the basis of secondary education, many of these skills are sorely missing. Take this list of ten skills and use it to develop a team that is ready for what is coming.

We live in the age of exponential change. Jobs — and indeed whole industries — are being made redundant. There will be more change in this generation than in the 200 years leading up to it. This is a fascinating idea, but what do we do with it? How do we react in the face of it? How do we evolve to keep ourselves relevant? How do we best prepare our children for the future?

Since the advent of traditional education forms, and the factory-like structures necessary to deliver them, there has been a huge focus on content-driven learning.

Reading, writing, and arithmetic have been favoured as the measurement of success. Students are tested on their ability to memorise knowledge above their ability to create it. As knowledge becomes freely available to the highest level of detail, and workplaces seek employees able to innovate and create, the skill sets that we currently value are not the ones that will take the next generation forward.

If reading, writing, and arithmetic are not enough for the future, what skills do we need to be developing instead? If you listen to the Australian Government, they are proclaiming a future that requires us to focus on Science, Technology, Engineering, and Mathematics.[1] This push is part of an initiative by the Department of Education and Training called Students First.[2] On the 7th December 2015, the Australian Government released the National Innovation and Science Agenda, with the core strategy being to inspire all Australians in digital literacy and STEM. In the USA we see a push towards coding and cognitive load coping. In Scandinavia, the Ashoka program[3] aims to connect and build 'changemaker schools' — schools that focus on developing the changemaker skills of empathy, creativity, leadership, and teamwork.

How do we evolve to keep ourselves relevant? How do we best prepare our children for the future?

Who else is talking? What are the trends from those with the foresight to plan for the future? Fast Company interviewed futurists and identified ten amazing future careers. These include Professional Tribers, Personal Brand Coaches and Urban Farmers. Check out the rest of their predictions on their website.[4] What's different about these, compared to the careers we currently see dominating the workforce?

The skill sets that we currently value are not the ones that will take the next generation forward

In *Meta Skills*, Marty Neumeier suggests a different set of skills. Neumeier is a past editor of Critique magazine and is an authority on design thinking. He starts his book with a statement coupled with a question. 'EEK a robot ate my job, now what?' He then continues to explore five meta skills he suggests we will need to thrive in the age of robots. These are; feeling, seeing, dreaming, making and learning. The fifth one — learning — positioned metaphorically as the opposable thumb of skills. Nice.

A group called the Institute for the Future, based at the University of Phoenix Research Institute, have addressed the question of future skills directly in their report Work Skills 2020.[5] Their list of skills is a result of a pretty impressive line up of thinkers in the space of change, disruption, and the future, including Steve Milovich from the Disney Corporation, Sonny Jandial from Procter and Gamble, and Micah Arnold from the Apollo Group. Their work identifies six drivers of change and ten skills we need to develop in response to those drivers (see Figure 13 on page 88).

Extreme longevity
Increasing global lifespans change the nature of careers and learning

Rise of smart machines and systems
Workplace automation nudges human workers out of rote, repetitive tasks

Computational world
Massive increases in sensors and processing power make the world a programmable system

New media ecology
New communication tools require new media literacies beyond text

Superstructured organisations
Social technologies drive new forms of production and value creation

Globally-connected world
Increased global interconnectivity puts diversity and adaptability at the centre of organisational operations

Figure 13.   Six drivers of change
Insititute for the Future

We can see how the Institute for the Future has used the drivers of change to form this list of ten skills for the future. Each skill is influenced by one or more drivers.

- **Sense making** — Ability to determine the deeper meaning or significance of what is being expressed

- **Social intelligence** — Ability to connect to others in a deep and direct way, to sense and stimulate reactions and desired interactions

- **Novel & adaptive thinking** — Proficiency at thinking and coming up with solutions and responses beyond that which is rote or rule-based

- **Cross-cultural competency** — Ability to operate in different cultural settings

- **Computational thinking** — Ability to translate vast amounts of data into abstract concepts and to understand data-based reasoning

- **New-media literacy** — Ability to critically assess and develop content that uses new media forms, and to leverage these media for persuasive communication

- **Transdisciplinary** — Literacy in and ability to understand concepts across multiple disciplines

- **Design mindset** — Ability to represent and develop tasks and work processes for desired outcomes

- **Cognitive load management** — Ability to discriminate and filter information for importance, and to understand how to maximise cognitive functioning using a variety of tools and techniques

- **Virtual collaboration** — Ability to work productively, drive engagement, and demonstrate presence as a member of a virtual team.

Trying to reduce these a little, I see three abstracted skills or capabilities that a business can focus on to create future value for their business (see Figure 14 on page 91).

These three skills help you develop creative solutions that take advantage of commercial opportunities and give you a competitive advantage. Get good at pattern recognition, get competent at value matching and use design thinking to drive innovation.

- **Pattern recognition** — similar to the idea of sense making, but with a bias towards data points and joining the dots for action. It's about seeing both the forest and the trees and creating an insight that drives change.

- **Value matching** — this is an idea rooted in client-centric business models, leadership engagement strategies, and good old-fashioned sales and marketing. We need to be able to connect value from one side to the other.

- **Innovative Design** — This is about making sure that what you do is solution-centred and directed towards affecting the human condition. Your work must make things better.

Which among these predictions will end up the most prescient? Of course, we cannot know. The key is to remember that what is most valuable today — those things that you (and your children) are put under pressure to focus on — will not be what is most valuable tomorrow.

If, as we look forward, we think about skills in terms of what we will need, not what is currently valued, then we have taken the first step to success in a changing world.

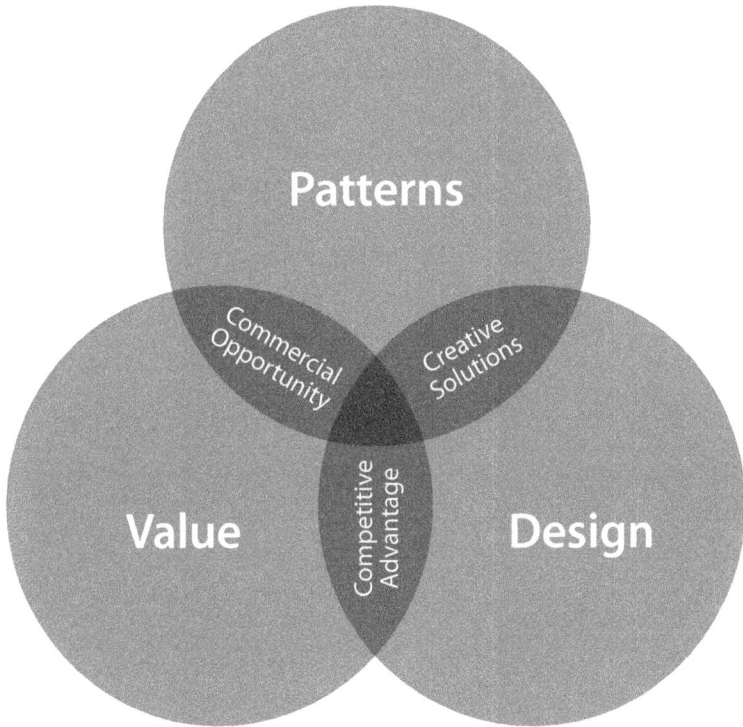

Figure 14. Future Value Creator

ONLINE REFERENCES

1. STEM Australia. http://www.stemaustralia.edu.au/

2. Australian Government Department of Education and Training Students First. 2016. *Students First*. https://www.studentsfirst.gov.au/

3. Ashoka. https://www.ashoka.org

4. Fast Company. 2015. *The Top Jobs in 10 Years Might Not Be What You Expect*. https://www.fastcompany.com/3046277/the-top-jobs-in-10-years-might-not-be-what-you-expect

5. Institute for the Future. 2011. *Future Work Skills 2020*. http://www.iftf.org/futureworkskills/

BOOKS MENTIONED

Neumeier, M., 2013. *Metaskills: Five Talents for the Robotic Age*. 1st ed. United States: New Riders.

DISCUSSION IDEAS

1 Review the 10 jobs for the future and see which ones might have your current role as DNA. This highlights what the evolution of your role is likely to be.

_____

_____

_____

2 Look at the 6 drivers for change and identify the #1 and #2 for your sector, industry or business unit.

_____

_____

_____

3 In small groups select 3 of the 10 future skills and define what they mean.

_____

_____

_____

4 Download the Work Skills 2020 report and pick one skill to delve deeper into. Commit to bringing a 10 minute presentation that summarises your research and unpacks how this skill could be developed in your team or business.

_____

_____

_____

EDUCATION 3.0

There is perhaps no greater example of the need to adapt than the drama playing out in the world of education. We know the system of education needs to change, we have research and clear evidence around the direction of change. We have champions who are inspiring and charismatic, and yet at a school near you very little is changing. This is a case study about the failure of an industry to shift, it's a case study on complexity and behavioural stubbornness. It's also possibly the key idea for driving change in your business — learning!

There was a time when teachers would teach the way they had learnt, with little regard to the needs of the student. The world changed when Howard Gardner and others came along and turned education on its head by promoting an agile teacher model. In this model the teacher — be they traditional classroom teachers or coaches, speakers or mentors — would adapt how they taught to meet the varying student needs.

But now a third wave is upon us, disrupting the existing pedagogies. This evolution of education is heralded by MOOCs (Massive Open Online Courses) provided by the likes of the Khan Academy.[1] Education is now about empowering the learner — not just through style, but also through access. And yet as I write, even the efficacy of MOOCS is coming into question.

While at first glance one would imagine the purpose of education is clear and easy to identify, if you canvass just a few people in your social network, I think you will realise the intent for education is not at all clear.

To be ready for an uncertain future we need to rely on a well-developed past. The purpose of education surely is to prepare us for tomorrow. But is it working? Does school prepare you for tomorrow? Are we building tomorrow's leaders today?

"We are currently preparing kids for jobs that do not exist yet, for technologies that have not been invented, to solve problems we don't even know are problems."

In the majority of cases, no. Our schools today are exam and content focused. Out of necessity — not a real necessity, mind you, but necessity driven by self-limiting structures — it targets the middle level, those students who aren't too brilliant and aren't too difficult. The comfortable ones to teach. It's based on a system of metrics and measurement, where we learn in classrooms, go home to practice, sit in rooms to be tested on standardised material (standardised to the middle, remember), and get ranked according to our 'abilities'. The focus is on standardisation and conformity, with a clear hierarchy from teachers to students. In essence, it's bureaucracy directed learning. The outcome now is to achieve high scores, not really to equip us for the workforce, not really to provide us with creative and open minds.

Randstad[2] conducted a study of employer confidence in education. The study was designed to see whether employers felt schools were preparing children for the future. The results were staggering, to a nation the employers had low levels of confidence in the schooling system. In every country measured the confidence was less than 50%, a fail by schooling's own measures.

> "The idea that our schools should remain content with equipping children with a body of knowledge is absurd and frightening. Tomorrow's adults will be faced with problems about the nature of which we can today have no conception. They will have to cope with the jobs not yet invented."

That was an article by Peter Mauger, printed in the magazine Forum: For the Discussion of New Trends in Education… in 1966. Over 50 years ago, leading educators looked at our education system and recognised that it no longer matched the environment it had been built for. Over 50 years ago it was recognised that we needed change. Only now is it finally starting to happen on a global scale. The pressure has been building for 50 years, and the release valve is now opening. Change is going to be rapid, and it's going to be massive.

Richard Riley, the former U.S. Secretary of Education, gave us the modern mantra about change with his statement:

> "We are currently preparing kids for jobs that do not exist yet, for technologies that have not been invented, to solve problems we don't even know are problems."

Why education needs to evolve to serve the new society

You can't offer a product that no longer matches the need. The need is no longer information. Therefore education is no longer about a transfer of information. 'What got you here won't get you there.'

There is so much untapped potential in individual children and areas as a whole. Take the story of 12-year-old Paloma and her class. Except, let's start with the teacher. Sergio Juárez Correa teaches in a school right on the border of Mexico and the US. It's on the Mexican side, which should give you an idea of the quality of life experienced by the children there. Tired of standing in front of the class talking at his students, Juárez Correa decided to trial a style of teaching he'd seen Sugata Mitra introduce on the internet — give students access not instruction. Give them problems, and stand back while they solve them. Give them freedom to choose what they learn. Give them curiosity.

If you feel that your business is not about education, you might be wrong.

A year later, the students had to sit the Mexican national standardised exam. Juárez Correa hated this style of standardised testing, but it was a requirement that couldn't be avoided. Two months later the results came out. Juárez Correa's class had gone from a 47% failure rate in maths to a 93% pass rate. A score ranked as Excellent had never been scored by any of these kids, yet 63% now hit that for maths. Ten students were in the 99.99th percentile. And the top score in the entire country had come from 12-year-old Paloma.

The press afterwards jumped on this story of genius kids living in the slums. Paloma, in particular, received a huge amount of attention for her phenomenal score. The opportunities that have been opened up for these kids is fantastic and deserved attention. And yet, the real point was completely missed. It was not that there were a bunch of genius kids living in the slums. These were normal kids, with normal variations in intelligence and learning speed. It was the style of teaching that had changed.

Ironically, Francisco Sánchez Salazar, the chief of the Regional Center for Educational Development in Matamoros, was publicly quoted soon after saying "The teaching method makes little difference."

We are in the most accelerated period of human development. Progress can only accelerate as quickly as education can allow it. Perhaps education is the only thing that can save the world.

The purpose of education

The purpose of education has evolved. It also differs slightly depending on whether you take the view of society, the educator, or the parents.

Parents initially used education as child-care as they moved off farms and into the industrial work environment. Then it was about capability teaching, providing skills and abilities that would serve them in later life. In more recent times, education has become the tool used to prepare them for the competitive nature of the workforce.

To be ready for an uncertain future we need to rely on a well-developed past. The purpose of education surely is to prepare us for tomorrow.

Educators used to work on a principle of severity at all times, as they imposed a set of standards and behaviours on children. Then it evolved into a focus of imprinting certain disciplines onto a child's brain. The future of education now is what the great teachers have aspired to throughout the ages — to inspire children to learn and use their talents.

Society has had different impacts on education as well; initially school was driven by religious interests, eventually it became more about government or political interest, and now it is in most cases about ensuring our people have an advantage on the world stage.

What's clear is that there is no single shaping force and that the parents, the educators, and the policy makers are not on the same page as to the purpose of school. If these purposes were aligned more directly, the framework to make education work brilliantly would be more effective.

Teachers can lead this charge, by embracing the new pedagogy (see Figure 15 on page 103).

EDUCATION 1.0

I'll deliver content at my pace and in my way, and you will learn if you can.

EDUCATION 2.0

I'll adjust how and what I teach so that it gives you the best chance for success.

EDUCATION 3.0

I'll provide you with the resources and content you need so you can learn what you need, in a way that works for you, whenever, and wherever you are. I will then make myself available to help you apply that learning in a useful manner.

PURPOSE OF EDUCATION

	1.0	2.0	3.0
PARENTS	Care	Capability	Competitive
EDUCATORS	Impose	Imprint	Inspire
SOCIETY	Driven by Religion	Driven by Government	Aiming for Advantage

Figure 15. The purpose of education
through three lenses

What's already happening

Salman Khan is now well known for his story of recording mathematics videos for his nephew, and from there progressing to supplying free educational videos to the entire world with the formation of the Khan Academy.

Sugata Mitra started with Hole in the Wall,[3] a revolutionary experiment where he placed a computer in a hole in the wall of his site in Delhi. Children from the adjoining slums had free access to learn and explore on this computer. They quickly learnt how to use not only the computer, but the programs and exercises that had been left on it.

The idea that our schools should remain content with equipping children with a body of knowledge is absurd and frightening.

From the success of this experiment, Mitra built School in the Cloud.[4] A Self Organised Learning Environment initiative, School in the Cloud connects children with a team of volunteer retired teachers — 'Grannies' — to supervise and answer questions. The children are challenged by the online environment to search out the answers to Big Questions and find their own way to creativity and knowledge acquisition.

Stanford University allowed Professor Sebastian Thruin and Peter Norvig to offer their course on Artificial Intelligence online for the first time in 2011. Enrolments went up from nearly 200 students the year before, to 160,000.

From New Delhi to New York, and the world of education to the world of investments. Salman Khan and the Khan Academy are signalling another major change in the world. As we are now one click away from much of the world's knowledge, perhaps the role of a teacher has shifted?

Thought leaders in education

The great Sir Ken Robinson is leading the education revolution. His book *Creative Schools* makes a compelling case and cites examples of education cultures from all over the globe that are responding to the 21ˢᵗ century needs of education. The most compelling ideas, in my opinion, are his suggestions around the end of systemised testing (NAPLAN are you listening?) and the shift from curriculum to disciplines.

I also love the work of David Gillespie, who suggests in his book *Free Schools* (useful if you live in Australia) that teacher mentoring is the key lever for educational transformation. Being the reformed lawyer that he is, he makes his case logically and with plenty of supporting evidence regarding the impact teachers make — both good and bad — on the progress of kids' learning. Principals who should have this as their primary work task are instead buried in administration, red tape, and bureaucracy as the government (at least here 'down under') continues to oversee the functioning of schools in an attempt to meet parent expectations and to create a 'best practice' that is anything but.

If you are in the business of educating others, you need to understand the changes and evolve.

I reckon all of us in the world of education need to analyse our practices and identify the ways we can improve. As stated earlier, the impact of these changes is not restricted to the traditional classroom teacher role. Speakers, authors, coaches, and trainers all need to analyse their delivery style and assess where improvements can be made. Are you embracing Education 3.0?

My response to this paradigm shift was the transformation of the delivery of the Thought Leaders practice methodology from a training session to an immersive program — Thought Leaders Business School.[5] This was a major departure from the traditional way we had been delivering this content for over 15 years. It required a great deal of research, development, and platform investment, not to mention a degree of faith in the efficacy of the new model of education.

Our faith was rewarded with the results for our students. Almost universally they have learned faster and implemented more effectively under the new model than the old. The impact of our work with them has been massively increased by embracing the disruption facing the world of education and making the decision to be at the forefront of this change. If you're in the business of educating others, I invite you to consider doing the same. And if you feel that your business is not about education, you might be wrong.

ONLINE REFERENCES

1. Khan Academy. https://www.khanacademy.org/

2. Randstad. https://www.randstad.com/

3. Hole in the Wall. http://www.hole-in-the-wall.com/

4. School in the Cloud. https://www.theschoolinthecloud.org/

5. Thought Leaders Business School. https://tlbusinessschool.com/

Fast Company. 2016. *The Flipped Classroom: Answering Obama's Call For Creativity in Education.* https://www.fastcompany.com/1679239/the-flipped-classroom-answering-obama-s-call-for-creativity-in-education

BOOKS MENTIONED

Gillespie, D., 2014. *Free Schools.* 1st ed. Australia: Macmillan Australia.

Robinson, K., 2015. *Creative Schools: The Grassroots Revolution That's Transforming Education.* 1st ed. United States: Viking

DISCUSSION IDEAS

1 What was your experience at school like?

_____

_____

_____

2 Of all the things you studied, what
do you still use today?

_____

_____

_____

3 Why do you think that is so?

_____

_____

_____

4 Why do you send your kids to school?

_____

_____

_____

5 If you created a school curriculum what new subjects would you introduce?

_____

_____

_____

6 Watch the TED video by Sugatra Mitra. How might the ideas he shares apply in your business?

_____

_____

_____

7 What business do schools think they are in?

_____

_____

_____

8 All this talk of education is interesting, but how does it apply to your role and your business?

_____

_____

_____

IF DA VINCI
HAD A WEBSITE

Your talented people need to be encouraged to build a portfolio of interests. Few of us are doing at work what we studied at university. You lose talent when you leave people working like a cog in the machine. This chapter explores how Leonardo da Vinci and Henry Ford might approach work and the personal branding of that work. It's about getting a project mindset going and allowing for some diversity in work.

The idea of specialisation or niching is a prevalent one. The argument goes that by focusing on one market or one expertise, you focus your efforts and get more done. I reckon it's an easy idea to swallow. Who hasn't felt diffused at some point, distracted by multiple angles and overwhelmed by many projects? The thing is I am not sure it's right for everyone or everything. It's convenient and functionally smart in business, but I don't think it's what genius does. A key competitive advantage we have in the developed world against the massive flow of people coming down the line from Brazil, Russia, India and China is to work in our genius.

I think that more and more people are shifting roles and jobs because they are looking to build a portfolio of interest. I suspect this one of the reasons great people leave your business. We put them in a box, square-cog them into the machine that is your organisational chart. Maybe if they had a wider variety of roles and projects, they would be more engaged. The bottom line is, give them what they are looking for and they might not leave, or at least as soon.

More and more people are shifting roles and jobs because they are looking to build a portfolio of interest.

Here is an old new idea — help them to be a renaissance man or woman, to be more like Leonardo da Vinci and less like Henry Ford. Ford is the poster child of the industrial revolution, and no doubt the emerging economies are visiting those heady days of resource and labour exploitation. But in countries with highly educated, developed, and sophisticated markets we need to step it up to a new level. We need to help them become innovation geniuses, dare I say thought leaders.

These new age geniuses need to be more like da Vinci, discovering new ideas at the edges of combined sciences and disciplines. Look up da Vinci on Wikipedia,[1] and it will list him as a renaissance

HENRY FORD	LEONARDO DA VINCI
Be Productive	Be Fulfilled
Fit In	Stand Out
Master of One	Master of Many
Do Work	Make Art

Figure 16.   Ford versus Da Vinci

polymath who worked as a botanist, an inventor, a biologist, an artist, a sculptor and in many, many more disciplines.

Thought leaders are inventors, not industrialists. Talented, smart people will need to be engaged like artists, not factory workers. Be careful what you believe and where you draw your inspiration when it comes to building a 21st-century organisation in the developed world.

Renaissance thinkers were most definitely multi-disciplinary. The formal name for their eclectic interest and diverse specialities was a polymath. I believe that thought leaders are polymaths or need to act like them. This is a big idea and one that requires you to invest mentally because it's counter cultural. It's not the story of our society right now, yet it is key to fixing a dilemma that many experts share. 'When I do so much, how do I answer the question, what do I do?'

These new age geniuses need to be more like Da Vinci, discovering new ideas at the edges of combined sciences and disciplines.

If this were a traditional book, I'd expand on the elements that contribute to this dilemma; there would be references to the industrial age and the push for specialisation, there would be a discussion about the flawed logic of niche marketing and it's inapplicability to the personal brands. There would be discussions about becoming fully expressed and self-actualised, and the negative impact narrowing has on this, but since this is just a single chapter in the book I'll get to the point.

Here is a case in point: as a thought leader, your personal website should showcase your width of knowledge. It should create a pattern of projects that once viewed, identify your expertise as a META idea, not a series of technical matters. Stay big and find a way to represent what you do that has integrity (you really are an expert in it), diversity (it's wide ranging in its applications), and self-expression (it's stuff that you are juiced by).

We are in such uncharted territory with this, because da Vinci and Michelangelo did not have websites. If they did, they most certainly would not be long-form sales letters focused on just one market. They would be portals of personality, showcasing a diverse thinker, with mastery in a number of disciplines and an essential recurring essence that appears in all that they do. Their ideas would evolve and be set up as projects that showcase what inspired them at a particular point in time. I think that Bill Gates' personal website is a great modern day example of this. Check out gatenotes.com.[2]

Their ideas would evolve and be set up as projects that showcase what inspired them at a particular point in time.

So da Vinci or Ford? This is the choice of *artist* versus *industrialist*. It may be a binary choice, but I know for sure which one is right for me!

ONLINE REFERENCES

1. Wikipedia. 2017. *Leonardo da Vinci.*
   https://en.wikipedia.org/wiki/Leonardo_da_Vinci

2. Gates Notes. 2017. *The Blog of Bill Gates.* https://www.gatesnotes.com/

DISCUSSION IDEAS

1 **What's the benefit of specialisation in your industry?**

_____

_____

_____

2 **Where could you get narrower?**

_____

_____

_____

3 **What does the term 'ruthless segmentation' mean to you?**

_____

_____

_____

4 **Have a discussion with people around you about whether you are using what you learnt at university in your current role.**

_____

_____

_____

5 What does the term trans-disciplinary mean to you?

_____

_____

_____

6 What is the next role or skill you
would want to develop?

_____

_____

_____

7 Research the word genius and think about whether
it applies to you? If so, where? If not, why?

_____

_____

_____

THE FOUR TEAMS

It's worth getting deliberate as a leader when you focus on the teams you are creating. Awareness of the different team types is your first step towards a better culture. Identifying where your players fit in is the next. With these two crucial pieces of information, you maximise your ability to build the optimum team. As a leader, decide what kind of team you want, recruit explicitly for that, and be the kind of leader that is required for each team.

break working environments into four team type: Elite, Functional, Family, and Floundering. Do you recognise what team you want to be a part of? And does that match your leadership style?

The key objective is to ensure that there's a match between the way you lead, and the team players. You can run a great Functional team, if everyone is aligned to this goal. Family teams are heart-warming and supportive, where individuals are open to the added closeness assumed in the group. An Elite team is an immensely powerful group, but it is absolutely vital that the trust and expectations have been set clearly so that everyone knows what the team is aspiring to. And the Floundering Team? Well, no one really wants to be a part of that team.

The key objective is to ensure that there's a match between the way you lead, and the team players.

Problems happen when there's no match between your leadership style and the team you've created. Your best and brightest may want to be part of an Elite team, but your leadership style is befitting to a Family team. These best performers can get equally annoyed at the mechanical attitude that Functional team players radiate. And Family team players will be exhausted if your leadership style creates an unrelenting competitiveness, more suited to an Elite team.

The key objective is to ensure that there's a match between the way you lead, and the team players.

I prefer to be part of an Elite team, because the games these teams play can be extraordinary. But it's not for everyone. Tensions arise if you are not clear about who is on your team, your expectations of them and the scope of your own role as their leader.

Let's review the four teams.

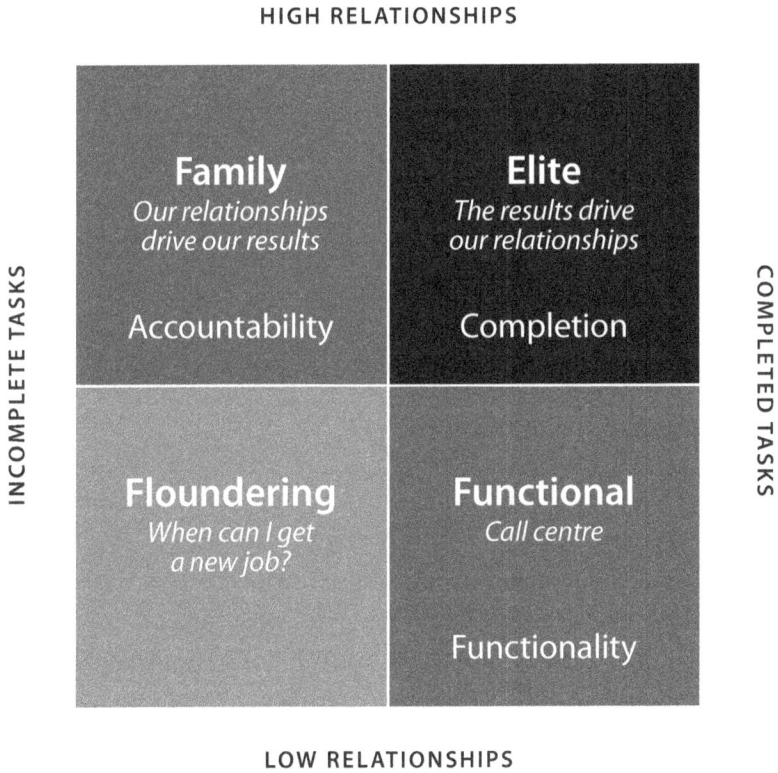

Figure 17. The four teams

FUNCTIONAL TEAM

A Functional Team gets the job done, but you won't really miss each other once the project's done or you move on. It's a polite, productive environment and as long as the work ticks all the relevant boxes; (convenient hours, close to home, OK money) people stay. This kind of team feels ordinary, and can exist for years simply getting things done. But don't expect people to work back, and don't ask them to come in early. Rather, it's a place where a certain set of tasks get done in a certain set of time. Small increases in pay are expected and overall the return is that you don't need to manage much. This kind of team attracts a certain personality type and has its place in the working landscape for now. But it's at risk with automation.

FAMILY TEAM

A Family Team feels like home. You cut people slack, forgive fast and have each other's back. Family teams are a place to grow, heal and spend time with each other, remember birthdays and go to the boss's for dinner. This kind of team feels safe and staff longevity is in abundance. In Family teams the leader invests considerable effort in improving the lives of those around them and people want to perform well to please the boss. The risk of this kind of team is that the dynamics present in your childhood may get triggered, resulting in people's traumas playing out at work. Leaders can also find themselves investing so much into their team members that they limit their own ability to make an impact.

ELITE TEAM

An Elite Team feels very different. Run like a high performance A-grade football team, you get cut when your performance drops and the pressure is unrelenting. There is huge pride and status to being part of this team. You get amazing things done and being a part of this unit feels exhilarating. Members of these teams need to work with a high level of initiative, and can't wait for the leader to give them every instruction. Leaders of these teams need to empower their staff to work autonomously, make decisions and take accountability. The risk of Elite teams is that good players can get left behind. If the expectations are higher than the quality of communication, then you'll struggle to find and keep good team members.

Leaders of Elite teams need to empower their staff to work autonomously, make decisions and take accountability.

FLOUNDERING TEAM

The fourth kind of team is the Floundering Team. No one really knows what they are doing, they can't seem to click, and most projects are seriously delayed. Typically a team flounders when the team type is not explicit, the leader's behaviour is not congruent to that type, or the rules of the game get muddled.

What kind of leader does each team need?

The thing is, as a leader, you need to know what kind of team you want. It talks to what kind of leader you will need to be.

If you ask yourself what the head of a Functional team feels like, the answer is Managerial; making sure the resources, systems and priorities are being followed.

The head of a Family team is parental in style. Lots of talking, lots of listening, helping people resolve their conflicts and making sure we all appreciate and value the differences in each other.

The head of an Elite team is focused, intense and pretty intolerant of excuses. They are driving ownership and accountability into every role and doing so from an evidence-based leadership perspective.

When someone feels like they are in a Family team, but the leader is driving an Elite performance, you get a clash.

When someone has a Functional attitude to their work and others have Family, relationship expectations get in the way.

The rules of the game

THE FUNCTIONAL BUSINESS

- Let's not get too emotional over this
- Fair day's work for a fair day's pay
- No surprises
- If it ain't broke, don't fix it
- That's XYZ's job — I'll let them know it came up
- Just keep things progressing
- Follow the rule book
- Play it safe
- Copy others in whenever you can [CC is your friend]
- Showing up is the job half done
- If in doubt, hold a meeting
- I don't have to like you to work with you

THE FAMILY BUSINESS

- Family first
- I have your back
- What we do here doesn't matter as much as who we are being here
- You don't sack family
- There is a time and a place for feedback
- The relationships at work are key to making work, work

- If you need someone to talk to, my door is always open

- If you drop the ball, I'll cover for you

- Business is personal

- What happens at home affects work, and vice versa

- Your dog and child are welcome here

- Work is a way of funding your life

THE ELITE TEAM

- It's not forever

- It's not for everyone

- Get your head in the game on game day

- Even if you are not playing, be at the game

- It's OK to drop the ball. It's not OK to do nothing about that

- I'm not your friend who's bossy, I'm a friendly boss

- Just turning up or dialing in are not OK here

- Your talent got you here; it's not enough to keep you here

- Going the extra mile is the cost of staying here

- When we meet, give me your performance review.
  Don't wait for me to tell you what needs work.

- Own your role and care about it more than I do.

- Leave the team a day early; rather than a day too late.

The Netflix manifesto has some interesting tonal qualities. Check out their culture document.[1] Now compare that to the equivalent from Tony Hsieg, CEO of Zappos,[2] and with the famous managers manual from Vault.[3]

Which of the three useful team cultures do each represent?

Problems happen when there's no match between your leadership style and the team you've created.

At Thought Leaders, my business partner Peter Cook and I are building a world-class education business, best practice.[4] This conversation around teams is one of our most important and challenging.

As a leader, decide what kind of team you want, recruit explicitly for that, and be the kind of leader that is required for each team.

Note: It's possible that pitch teams, creative teams, and leadership teams operate in different models to these; every model is useful, until it's not. Use this framework to plan an intentional team culture and get very explicit about what you want from the people on your team.

ONLINE REFERENCES

1. Netflix. 2017. *Life at Netflix.* https://jobs.netflix.com/life-at-netflix

2. About Zappos Culture | Zappos.com. 2017.
   http://www.zappos.com/core-values

3. The Vault. 2017. *The Vault Managers Manual.*
   http://www.vapethevault.com/managersmanual/

4. Thought Leaders Business School. https://tlbusinessschool.com/

DISCUSSION IDEAS

1 What kind of team are you part of?

_____
_____
_____

2 What kind of leader are you?

_____
_____
_____

3 Are you cool with that, or do you want to make a different choice?

_____
_____
_____

4 Review the functional team rules of the game and have a discussion with others about what you think of this list.

_____
_____
_____

5 Can you add any more?

_____

_____

_____

6 Review the family team rules of the game and have a
discussion with others about what you think of this list.

_____

_____

_____

7 Can you add any more?

_____

_____

_____

8 Review the elite team rules of the game and have a
discussion with others about what you think of this list.

_____

_____

_____

9 Can you add any more?

_____

_____

_____

ENTERPRISING THOUGHT LEADERSHIP

Retaining and attracting the best and brightest has to be one of your biggest challenges. You can pay your employees well, promote them to more senior roles, and recognise their efforts with bonuses and development opportunities. For many of your employees, this will be sufficient. However, your best and brightest are looking for something more. They want to belong to something different, to give back, they want to leave a legacy. They may not work with you forever, but they want to say "I did this when I worked there."

The challenge of becoming an employer of choice means you are fighting a war on on two fronts, one facing out and one in. The first, attracting and retaining clients, the second; running a campaign to engage your best and brightest.

Business needs to undertake a new leadership imperative. We need to develop internal thought leaders and as a result create a competitive advantage. This is not something conducted across the whole organisation, but it will affect the whole organisation. This is not something that marketing is responsible for, but it will drive better positioning and brand awareness. This is not something for HR to direct as a people issue, although it will most definitely engage your high potentials better than any offsite ever could. This is first and foremost a strategic leadership issue.

The challenge of becoming an employer of choice means you are fighting on two fronts: new clients and a campaign to engage your best and brightest.

The three big challenges

I see three challenges that are slowing down large organisations. Three areas where you can gain a competitive edge if you develop a small team of thought leaders.

The first is the war for talent, the second is the battle for attention, and the third is winning the race to the future (see Figure 18 on page 133).

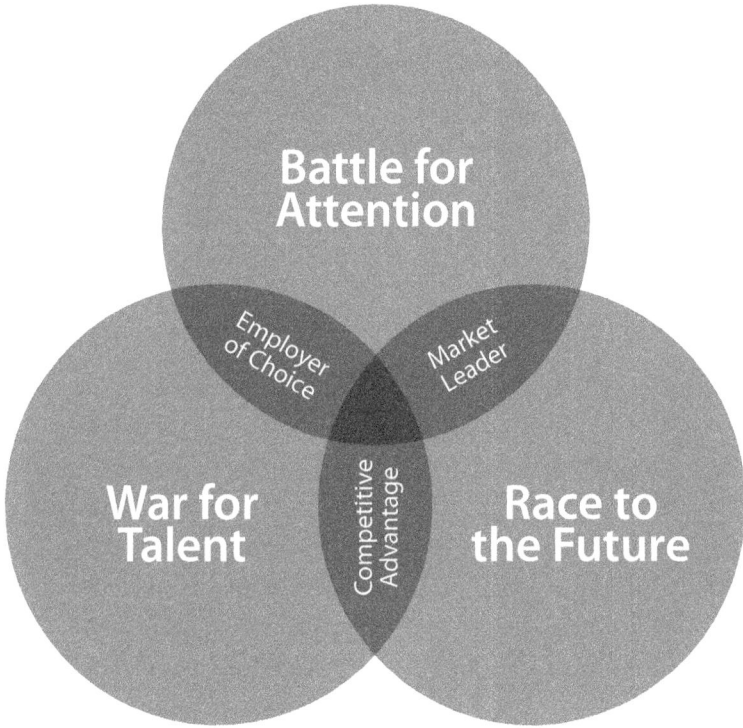

Figure 18. The three challenges

THE WAR FOR TALENT

Build capacity, not capability

Putting your smart people into training courses is not going to end well.

Talented people want to manage their professional development; compliance based courses and ineffective training are not the solutions they need. They need to be inspired to be inspiring. This is one of the hidden levers of developing your thought leaders. Work hard on the role modelling and the internal status of the thought leaders in your business. The examples they set — speaking at client conferences, leading internal meetings and publishing insights — become major rallying calls for others in the organisation to step up and shine (see Figure 19 on page 135).

These subject matter experts are ideally admired by others in your industry due to their ability to capture, package, and deliver great ideas.

Retaining and attracting the best and brightest has to be one of your biggest challenges. You can pay your employees well, promote them to more senior roles and recognise their efforts with bonuses and development opportunities. For many of your employees, this will be sufficient. However, your best and brightest are looking for something more. They've grown past simply wanting to improve themselves, or to contribute to a workplace. Their sense of purpose has matured to the extent that they want to leave a legacy. This is where you have to reach them.

THE BATTLE FOR ATTENTION

Traditional marketing is dead

As the return on investment from traditional marketing channels continues to decline, everyone from senior executives to small business owners are now scrambling to find the next way to market their

3–5min **On a Panel**

15min **Napkin at Cafe**

20min **TED-style talk**

30min **Lunch and Learn**

90min **Session at Industry Conference**

1day **Offsite**

90sec **Media Release**

3min **Video Insight**

750w **Article in Journal**

4,000w **Chapter in Book**

5,000w **White paper / Report**

40,000w **Book**

Figure 19. Where you can use your thought leaders to share their points of view and insights.

services and products to their customers. Digital marketing, including social media, has exploded, with some companies embracing this completely while others are just 'testing the waters' to see what this approach will bring in real sales to their business, not just a number of likes and positive comments on Facebook.

The need to stand out in your market has never been stronger than it is today. So how can you position your business as being individual and different from everyone else trying to promote their unique value proposition?' How can you find the edge for your business and be seen and heard over the noise? By positioning your business as the thought leader in your industry, you will be seen as leading edge and will attract customers organically. This doesn't replace marketing; it supports sales! (see Figure 20 on page 137)

Below the line on this model is the traditional Push activities. 'Marketing', 'selling' to new clients and selling more products to existing clients through 'relationships'. These are all effective, and yet they all require a certain 'push' onto the market. A business that takes the time to make marketing effective by formalising their sales funnels and nurture existing relationships has a solid business development process. It does take continuous effort though.

Above the line on this model are the Pull activities. Businesses and professions that tend to do less marketing, for example, professional service firms or professions like law, will traditionally rely on these more. Generally over time, as you deliver great work, you build a reputation that drives future business. The first of these is a straight up 'referral': being so good for so long that people start saying "Don't even think of doing X until you talk to Y". Above this is the idea of getting serious about distribution partners and channel relationships. The big idea, the one that trumps all the previous, is being known for knowing something. Once individuals, and by default the business, are positioned as thought leaders the game tilts in your favour. When this tilt happens you get a significant competitive edge in the marketplace.

MARKET POSITION

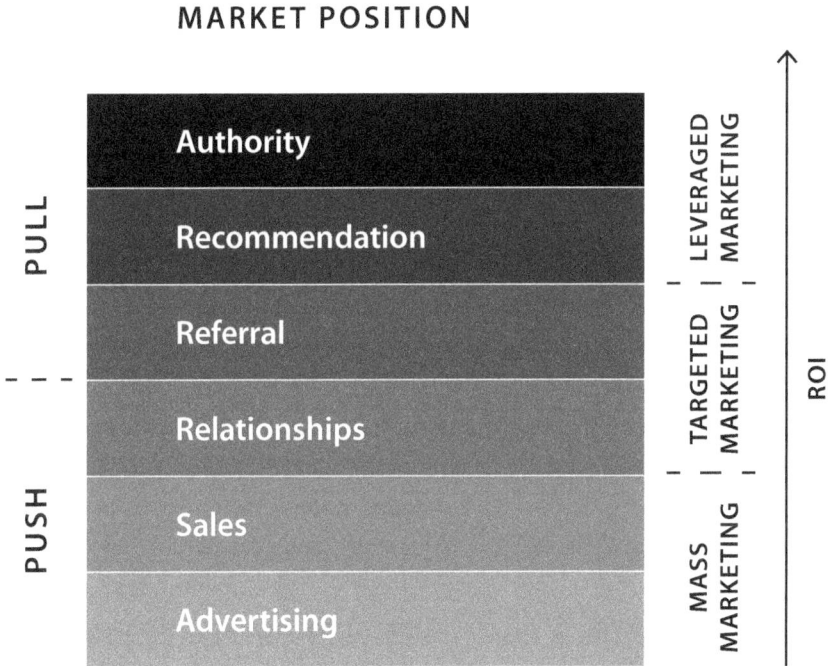

Figure 20. Push versus Pull Business Growth Strategies

THE RACE TO THE FUTURE

Innovation comes from within

What got you here may not get you there. As evidenced through-out history, both ancient and recent, it's incredibly hard to change a system when you're living within the system. For those operating in large, complex organisational structures with many moving parts, leading change and disruption is incredibly difficult. Essentially, past successes lull organisations into continuing blindly along the same path, discouraging adaptation to new circumstances.

A small team of thought leaders can ask the tough questions, challenge the status quo, put the sacred cows out to pasture, and do so without removing the momentum of the current business. They can develop the dangerous ideas you need in your business if you're going to shift towards the future. A dream team of thought leaders gives you the edge to disrupt yourself.

Corridor doubt is an awful thing. Imagine we have had a meeting in which we discussed the benefits of thought leadership. It all made sense at the time, but then in the corridor, you whisper "But are any of our people thought leaders?" This happens more often than any of us would like to admit. The 'not good enough' paradigm raises its ugly head. Ben Zander said it brilliantly in his ground-breaking TED talk of 2005: "A leader must never doubt the ability of their people to realise whatever they are imagining."[1] This doubt is the impostor syndrome turned non-specific. It is false, and it's not helpful. You have thought leaders; you just don't know it yet. Develop your talent and watch them fly.

Develop a small team of thought leaders to drive change.

Do this well, and you increase the chances that you will win the race to the future.

So how does a business enterprise thought leadership?

There are a number of ways to get your business positioned as a thought leader or leading authority in your industry. Many marketing gurus obsess about creating a brand that has a personality. This is to make a business feel more like a person than a business. One of the reasons for this line of thinking is that people trust individuals more than faceless companies. If a brand has a personality that is attractive, it creates followers who are more committed and loyal than typical customers. To position your business as a thought leader, you need to have some individuals that become known for being the leading thinkers in your industry. These subject matter experts are ideally admired by others in your industry, due to their ability to capture, package, and deliver great ideas with others.

ONLINE REFERENCES

1. Benjamin Zander, *The Transformative Power of Classical Music.*
   https://www.ted.com/talks/benjamin_zander_on_music_and_passion

DISCUSSION IDEAS

1 **Who is a thought leader in your industry?**

_____
_____
_____

2 **Who within your business might already be considered a thought leaders?**

_____
_____
_____

3 **Is this something for the whole business or a select few?**

_____
_____
_____

4 **Who is your go-to person to speak at client events?**

_____
_____
_____

5 What annual event do you run that positions
your staff as subject matter experts?

_____

_____

_____

6 When your team speak are they pushing products
and services, or educating the market?

_____

_____

_____

7 If your company published a book of
insights each year, what would the chapters
be and who would write each one?

_____

_____

_____

8 Using the ideas in Figure 19, identify 3 opportunities
to show up as a thought leader in the next 90 days.

_____

_____

_____

THE IMPLEMENTATION REVOLUTION

We need to become obsessed with getting things done. Moving from talking and meeting to actually doing. This shift requires a more entrepreneurial than employee mindset. There needs to be a bias for action and a commitment to results. This chapter creates some reference points for getting more people more committed to getting more done in your business.

Google Inc recently changed its name and structure to Alphabet Inc.[1] The company's mission as Google Inc was to organise all the information on the planet, and while that's still true of Google the search company, the Alphabet mission is about "getting more ambitious things done."

This shift is a major turning point in the world-changing business that was Google Inc. It's a widening of purpose around the idea of realising ambitious projects. It's symbolic of this first major revolution, this major technological revolution; the shift from information to implementation. Things like self-driving cars and aircraft, improving transportation efficiency, gaining a greater understanding of health and disease, extending lifespans, creating environmentally friendly distributed energy grids.

Larry Page says this in his letter to the stockmarket around the restructure from Google Inc to Alphabet Inc: "We've long believed that over time companies tend to get comfortable doing the same thing, just making incremental changes. But in the technology industry, where revolutionary ideas drive the next big growth areas, you need to be a bit uncomfortable to stay relevant."

The driver behind these trends is the positive aspiration of increasing freedom for humans.

Eric Schmidt from Google, in his thorough tomb of a book *How Google Works,* outlines that the internet has been built by two billion people like you and me — well educated, somewhat privileged individuals living in a developed nation. He and his co-author Jonathan Roseberg predict that over the next few years a further four billion users will come online and start to reshape the internet as we know it. These four billion users will have new demands and potentially stronger drives to engage with the internet in a new way.

It's symbolic of this first major revolution, the shift from information to implementation. My friend and business partner Peter Cook

Alphabet

Google

Google
Search, Apps, Maps,
Android

X
Self-driving cars & aircraft,
space-based internet
network, wind energy

Calico

Calico
Biology & ageing

Jigsaw

Jigsaw
Tech solutions for global
problems

verily

Verily
Life sciences and
technology

nest

Nest
Home automation

SIDE WALK LABS

Side Walk Labs
Tech solutions for urban
environments

Google Fiber

Fiber
Fibre-To-The-Premises
internet

GV

GV & Google Capital
Venture capital firms

Figure 21.   Alphabet makes Google's mission broader

wrote a great book about the shift from tasks to projects, with a clear action plan for building a bias towards getting things done. Read *The New Rules of Management.*

The origin of the internet can be taken back to universities, the particle accelerator at CERN,[2] and the need for researchers to share large amounts of information quickly. It quickly got away from its creators, going from 'significant and available to a few' to 'shallow and available to the masses' (at least the privileged masses), all so we could share memes like cappuccino art and cat videos. Possibly its most out-of-control use is as a source of pornography distribution.

So what's next? Is social media the new internet? Will we end up with internet 2.0? What will it look like, what will it enable? The internet is only one technology, but the shift we are experiencing there and in other domains is one from information warehousing to one that enables things to happen. From ideas to implementation.

This is the key; it's about getting stuff done. Meaningful stuff.

I see three big technologies shifting and colliding, and the impact of these shifts will be felt across industry, beyond borders and into the lives of all of us (see Figure 22 on page 147).

The Internet of Things is a term for the connectivity of devices. Big data is the mining of behaviour, so we can build profiles on what people do and at some level predict what they want to do next. The third big technology coming our way is Artificial intelligence. Think robots and more!

Even more important than these technologies alone is their impact when combined with each other. Consider the intersection of the Internet of Things and Big Data. Everything around us knowing everything about us will make marketing more relevant and mean-ingful. Think traffic lights that slow down cars and reroute commuter traffic when accidents appear. Think customised television ads based on internet search history. Of course, it's hard to keep skeletons hid-den in the closet or have secrets from society, when this is the level of data sharing and retention. Are secrets a good thing or a bad thing? That's a complicated discussion that we'll save for another time.

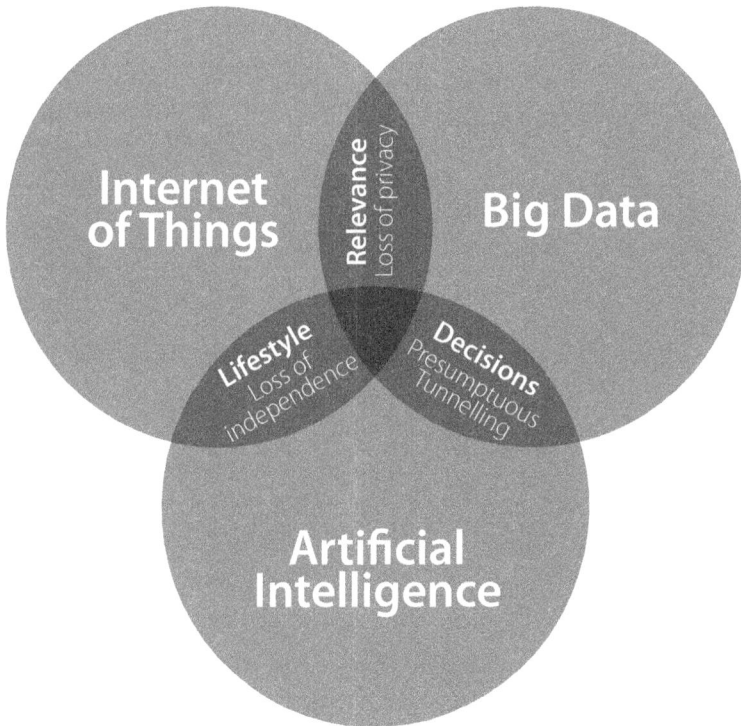

Figure 22.   The three forces of change

Consider the intersection of the Internet of Things and Artificial Intelligence. A robot that's connected to our house should make our life easier, though we might lose the independence and freedom of choice. You might enjoy your coffee brewing ritual in the morning and having this mundane task taken off you could lead to a lowered sense of satisfaction. There are both benefits and consequences to going down these pathways that we cannot even imagine now.

This is the key; it's about getting stuff done. Meaningful stuff.

Consider the intersection of the Artificial Intelligence and Big Data. A robot that knows our preferences could make decisions for us that we like. Self-driving cars that can negotiate the best routes through traffic, communicate with the other vehicles on the road, and park themselves while you're in your meeting.

The driver behind these trends is the positive aspiration of increasing freedom for humans. The risk will be a potential loss of liberty. Conversations in this space quickly degenerate into bad sci fi movies with a dystopian view of the world of robots. Whether it's an Arnold Schwarzenegger Terminator vibe with Skynet pushing humans underground like roaches, or the Spike Jones epic robot love fest 'She', we see views of a future world where the very technology we developed to set us free imprisons us. As easy as it may be to dismiss these views as cheap Hollywood entertainment, some serious players are exploring with some paranoia the risks we take as these new technologies collide and change the very fabric of how we live and work.

Nick Bostrom, articulates the AI future challenge well in his Ted talk.[3]

Elon Musk, the revolutionary entrepreneur, founder of Tesla,[4] and champion of Space X,[5] last year founded Open AI,[6] a not for profit on a mission. Its mission statement is "OpenAI is a non-profit artificial intelligence research company. Our goal is to advance digital intelligence in the way that is most likely to benefit humanity as a whole, unconstrained by a need to generate a financial return." Essentially, he has gathered some of the world's leading artificial intelligence engineers and set them the mission of driving advancement in artificial intelligence. Doing so in an open-source, give-it-all-away culture. The hope is that rather than shying away from the evolutions in this space, the solution lies in running towards it in an aboveground, crowd-sourced fashion. His sense is that this is something too big to leave in the hands of a profit-oriented company structure.

In a nutshell: If knowledge is information, wisdom is the understanding and application of that knowledge, and insight is the awareness of the underlying essence of a truth.

Larry Page and Sergey Brin, in pursuing transparency with the structure of Alphabet Inc, and Elon Musk with the formation of OpenAI, are showing a leadership towards future structures that have accountability, and a higher level of intent than simply returning value to shareholders.

What does all this mean for your career, your projects and your businesses? The movement from information to implementation is creating some forces for change.

Wisdom, knowledge and insight are not the same things. Royale Scuderie[7] is a contributing author at Lifehack and the president of Productive Life Concepts.[8] She defines these three terms beautifully:

> Knowledge is the accumulation of facts and data that you have learned about or experienced. It's being aware of something and having information. Knowledge is really about facts and ideas that we acquire through study, research, investigation, observation, or experience.
>
> Wisdom is the ability to discern and judge which aspects of that knowledge are true, right, lasting, and applicable to your life. It's the

ability to apply that knowledge to the greater scheme of life. It's also deeper; knowing the meaning or reason; about knowing why something is, and what it means to your life.

Insight is the deepest level of knowing and the most meaningful to your life. Insight is a deeper and clearer perception of life, of knowledge, of wisdom. It's grasping the underlying nature of knowledge, and the essence of wisdom. Insight is a truer understanding of your life and the bigger picture of how things intertwine.

In a nutshell: If knowledge is information, wisdom is the understanding and application of that knowledge and insight is the awareness of the underlying essence of a truth.

Key Takeaway

This shift from knowing something, to discerning the useful bits, to ultimately applying that knowledge and judgement to a particular benefit, is absolutely key.

This is essentially a process, not just a language distinction. The process is one of answering three questions when looking at any idea or project:

1. What's going on? (knowledge)

2. What does it mean? (wisdom)

3. How can we use that to make something happen? (insight)

Technology is changing our lives, and it's not going to be through the colour or size of your iPhone. It's not even going to be a watch that tells more than the time. What it's really about is what happens with all that connectivity, tracking, and information, as we continue intertwining technology more and more in our lives.

ONLINE REFERENCES

1. Alphabet. 2017. *G is for Google.* https://abc.xyz

2. CERN. 2017. *CERN Accelerating Science.* https://home.cern

3. TED. 2015. *Nick Bostrom: What happens when our computers get smarter than we are?.* https://www.ted.com/talks/nick_bostrom_what_happens_when_our_computers_get_smarter_than_we_are

4. Tesla. 2017. *Elon Musk.* https://www.tesla.com/elon-musk

5. SpaceX. 2017. http://www.spacex.com

6. OpenAI. 2017. *Discovering and enacting the path to safe artificial general intelligence.* https://openai.com

7. Lifehack. 2017. *Royale Scuderi.* http://www.lifehack.org/author/rscuderi

8. BlogHer. 2017. *Productive Life Concepts.* http://www.blogher.com/productive-life-concepts

9. Wikipedia. 2017. *BRIC.* https://en.wikipedia.org/wiki/BRIC

BOOKS MENTIONED

Cook, P., 2013. *The New Rules of Management: How to Revolutionise Productivity, Innovation and Engagement by Implementing Projects That Matter.* 1st ed. Australia: John Wiley & Sons Australia, Ltd.

Schmidt, E., 2014. *How Google Works.* 1st ed. United States: Grand Central Publishing

DISCUSSION IDEAS

1 **What do you think of the shift in mission statement and name from Google to Alphabet?**

_____
_____
_____

2 **What is the mission of your business?**

_____
_____
_____

3 **Watch Simon Sinek's 'Start with Why' TED talk and answer the What, How and Why of your business.**

_____
_____
_____

4 **What are the top three frictions when doing business with you, and what is your business doing about them right now?**

_____
_____
_____

5 How good are you personally at starting things?

_____

_____

_____

6 How good are you at finishing things?

_____

_____

_____

7 Where have you used a personal project to get something amazing done in your life?

_____

_____

_____

8 Could any of the elements in that project be used at work to advance your wildly important goals?

_____

_____

_____

THE FOUR ENEMIES OF GREAT WORK

This chapter is focused on calling out the four things that are stopping us from doing great work. As I see it, these are the four enemies to great work: email, meetings, Powerpoint and politics. Email is wearing busy people down. Meetings are killing us. Powerpoint is putting us to sleep. Politics is slowing us all down. Work hard on removing these enemies from the battlefield, and work that was previously a grind can become work that is great.

A common theme in my work revolves around the idea of getting fit for the future. It's about exploring what we can do to enhance our lives and our work as we head into the decade of disruption. Often the future will need us to have some new capabilities; like sense making, novel thinking or social intelligence. Sometimes it's about capacity management; being fitter or removing the frictions or things that get in our way. This chapter is about capacity — and more specifically the capacity drain that email, meetings, Powerpoint and politics are causing in our teams and businesses. There are not enough hours in the day to achieve balance and enjoy progress if we are always in meetings, interrupted by memos, or managing the agendas of those invested in the status quo.

All great businesses and teams have leaders worth following, cultures worth belonging to, and work worth doing. But if we let the mechanical nature of work stunt the creative flow and the Machiavellian nature of humans take over, then our greatest work is at risk.

We need email and meetings to make progress visible, not to exist simply to demonstrate a form of 'busyness'.

As I see it, there are four enemies to great work. Four dynamics at play that stop us from being our best, whether that be personally or collectively. These four frictions create stress, eat up our day and emotionally exhaust us. By consciously removing these enemies, we clear a path for an effective action-based work flow. In other words, work works, rather than it becoming a sequence of chores that turn into a daily grind.

Here are four dynamics at play that stop us being our best.

1. Email

It's wearing us down. We need to focus more on our priorities and ignore the pull of checking the most recent message every few minutes.

2. Meetings

They're killing us. They need to be intentional and something we use as a tool rather than a habit.

3. Powerpoint

It's putting us to sleep. It's a great as a preparation tool, but boring as a presentation format.

4. Politics

Office politics are slowing us down. Leaders need to spend less time managing their image and more time making an impact.

Here is how they work together to drain the desire to create in your best people. The first three are mechanical, dealing with the actual tools we use to run our business. The last is personal, dealing with interactions between individuals, and the intent behind it. This is how they kill innovation, drive culture in the wrong direction and reward the wrong behaviours in our teams and businesses.

We need meetings and Powerpoint to inspire us, not simply inform us.

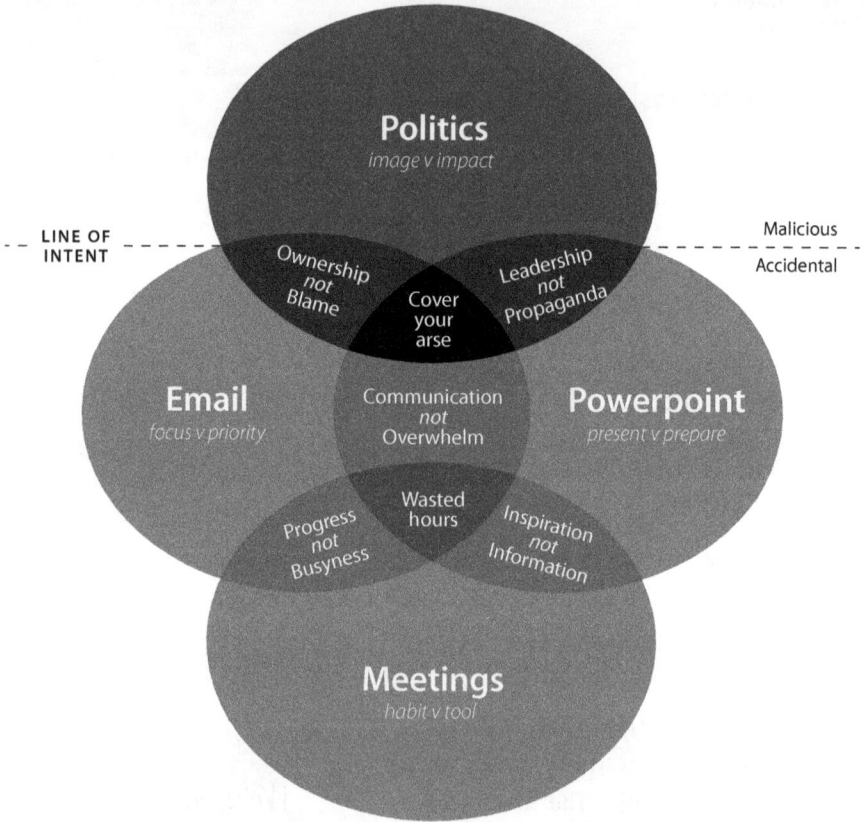

Figure 23. The four enemies of great work

Unpacking the model

The Line of Intent that divides the model speaks to how the enemies have evolved over time, like rust on an old engine. Often the rust is holding the engine brackets together, and by scrubbing at them, you expose weakness. By focusing on emails, meetings and Powerpoint and scrubbing away the old unhelpful stuff you often expose a weakness in the structure of the business. e.g. some of the people you pay to turn up don't get anything done. This entropic build-up of inefficiencies is what happens mostly below the line of intent. Above the line things are more Machiavellian; when an unhelpful political drive sits maliciously over the three mechanical enemies it's harder to scrub away the rust and expose the underlying weakness. When people are covering their arse, spending time on the politics of work and using meetings, emails and Powerpoint to advance propaganda, the great game of work gets harder to play.

Work comes before email. Be cognizant of what needs to get done and do that first.

Staying below the line for a moment, we need email and meetings to make progress visible, not to simply exist to demonstrate a form of 'busyness'. We need meetings and Powerpoint to inspire us, not simply inform us. Emails and PowerPoint are not communicating if they are simply overwhelming the recipient. Our job as a leader is not to dump information on others; it's to make sure they understand. The onus is on you as the leader to communicate well, not on your people to get across your stuff.

Above the line, we need to drive ownership and accountability, not blame, and we need more leaders doing things, having an impact and not simply pushing agendas or propagating their personal points of view.

Essentially, politics is more about how something looks, and less about the impact made on real issues. Make a decision, make progress visible, drive ownership not blame.

Email is not an insurance policy, nor is it a to-do list. When your day is driven by the content of your inbox, you are putting out fires and allowing other's urgency to drive your work flow. Work comes before email. Be cognizant of what needs to get done and do that first. Email is sometimes a way of covering your arse. If you CC as a way of passing the buck, it's a professional form of passive aggressive behaviour. If you BCC instead of having transparent conversations, you might be playing politics. Email is not a substitute for conversation. Maybe instead, pick up the phone or walk down the hall to a colleague's desk.

Lead.
Let's make some decisions
without covering our arses.

Meetings have become habits and not tools for change. (Read more about meetings as tools in Chapter 160. Elemental Meetings, starting on page 160). Bottom line: Don't be at one if you don't have to be. Don't make them 30 minutes by default. Don't let anyone add an item to the agenda that was not there previously. And get clear what you want as an outcome at the end of the meeting before it even starts.

Powerpoint should be something you use to prepare a talk, but not necessarily something you use to present a talk. In your next meeting try presenting without Powerpoint on the screen. Maybe tell a story instead. If you have to use slides, replace the bullet points with images. Then use the bullet points as presenter notes, not audience visuals.

Fortunately, there are simple fixes to dealing with each enemy. They only take a small amount of effort, but they do require a strong dose of commitment.

EMAIL

1. Check it at set times only. If it's urgent, they'll call you.

2. Be brief. If it can't be brief, make a call.

3. Don't let your inbox set your priorities.

MEETINGS

1. Make sure you're only at meetings that matter. Halve your meetings.

2. Initiate or attend only the right type of meeting based on your goal (see Chapter 161. Elemental Meetings, starting on page 161, for more).

3. Don't let people waste their time or yours.

POWERPOINT

1. Use bullet lists for presenter notes, not audience slides.

2. Put images on your slides, not text.

3. Tell stories, don't recite words.

POLITICS

1. Sit in circles so there is no status.

2. Speak last and allow others to express their point of view.

3. Make a decision. In all gatherings ask yourself 'What question are we discussing? What decision are we making?

So in summary, to counter these enemies we need to:

1. Pick up the phone

2. Know what we want out of a meeting

3. Tell stories rather than read Powerpoint slides; and,

4. Lead. Let's make some decisions without covering our arses.

I get it's not easy, but as Stephen Pressfield says in the *War of Art*, art is hard. He calls it the resistance, it's a war against procrastination and inertia. These enemies make the great work—the art—very difficult. Fight these four enemies and win the battle against email, Powerpoint and meetings. Watch out for those invested in the status quo as their politics will drive your business and projects down the disruption drain.

📖 BOOKS MENTIONED

Pressfield, S., 2002. *The War of Art: Break Through the Blocks and Win Your Inner Creative Battles.* 1st ed. United States: Rugged Land, LLC.

DISCUSSION IDEAS

1 Discuss a project that's stalled in your business, name it but don't go too deep yet.

_____
_____
_____

2 Now ask yourself which of the three mechanical enemies are the front line in your business?

_____
_____
_____

3 What could you do about that today?

_____
_____
_____

4 Have a discussion about the line of intent and mechanical versus machiavellian intent.

_____
_____
_____

5 Does your business have a brevity guideline around email?

_____

_____

_____

6 Does your business have a policy around who must attend meetings?

_____

_____

_____

7 What's the number one tip you can share about handling each of the four enemies?

_____

_____

_____

8 Collate everyone's tips and decide how to share these with the wider organisation.

_____

_____

_____

ELEMENTAL MEETINGS

We spend so much time in meetings. They are not liked by most who attend and few rate them as effective. Yet we keep doing them, why? We meet to create joint ventures, negotiate deals or simply to get things done. There are a lot of really good reasons to meet, but so few meetings live up to their potential. Lets explore in this chapter how to turn meetings from time wasters into agents of change.

've been thinking a lot about meetings; how much time we waste in them and how bad we are at running them. From the small meetings with mentors for advice, to the big meetings we call conferences. We meet to create joint ventures, negotiate deals, or simply to get things done. There are a lot of really good reasons to meet, so why do so few meetings live up to their potential?

Basically, as a whole, we are really bad at meetings. But could we turn them around? Could we take them from time wasters to extraordinary agents of change?

If you ask any executive leading a large organisation, they will tell you that huge swaths of their time are taken up in poorly run meetings that suck time and cause extraordinary opportunity loss. In an era when our time is probably one of the top three resources we have, we are squandering it in bad collaborations called meetings. As a result, we say "We are not aligned", "They are not engaged", or "We need to work on our team building." This may all be true, but I reckon we jump to prescribe these bigger issue fixes when maybe, just maybe, all we need to do is better define why we are meeting.

Getting good at meetings —the primary agent of change—is a big idea.

The problem is we call meetings without being clear on why or what we want to achieve, and then treat all meetings as equal when they might be served by different structures and procedures. Take for example a meeting to discuss speakers for a conference. There is a degree of brainstorming required, but ultimately this meeting needs to reach a decision. Which of the five speakers will be engaged and why?

Planning a conference requires you to get clear on some key objectives to answer some basic questions: the meta question being, "What do you hope to achieve out of this conference?" and then specifically "Is there a gap in our line up of speakers?" Having run events for several years and been a speaker for consideration more times than I count, it helps to see this as two meetings: the first one of awareness — exploring choices — and the second one of decisions — closing down choices.

I created this model to explain to conference committees the different goals of events and different types of speakers you can engage to meet those needs (see Figure 24 on page 170).

Al Pittampalli, a graduate of Seth Godin's Alternative MBA Program,[1] has written a manifesto titled *Read This Before Our Next Meeting*. You can watch Al make his hypothesis in the video referenced at the end of this chapter,[2] and you can read a quick summary as well.

In his manifesto, he proposes that there are two types of meetings: 'decision making' meetings where the only thing done is the discussion on that topic and 'brainstorming' meetings where we ideate new solutions. He calls his approach the modern meeting solution. It includes some really good ideas for how we decide whether we need to participate in a meeting or not, and if we do, what are the rules of engagement? Things like 'Don't attend a meeting if you don't have to' and 'Don't turn up late' and 'If you have not read the pre meeting notes you can't attend.'

I liked the simplicity of his hypothesis; "There are only two types of meetings", but I wondered if it was true?

It's not.

It is useful, but it's incomplete. Those two meeting types are helpful, but in no way are they collectively exhaustive or practically useful when there are at least four other meeting types.

Have you ever caught up with someone to build a relationship? Have you ever caught up with someone to get their advice? Both are types of meetings, but neither fit the 'decision making' or 'brainstorming' definition of a meeting.

This got me thinking about the different types of meetings we have and the fact that maybe if we got clear on our choices and the operating guidelines for these meetings, we might be more effective at having meetings. We all agree that meetings are not working, I reckon we have a universal consensus on that. Put simply; meetings

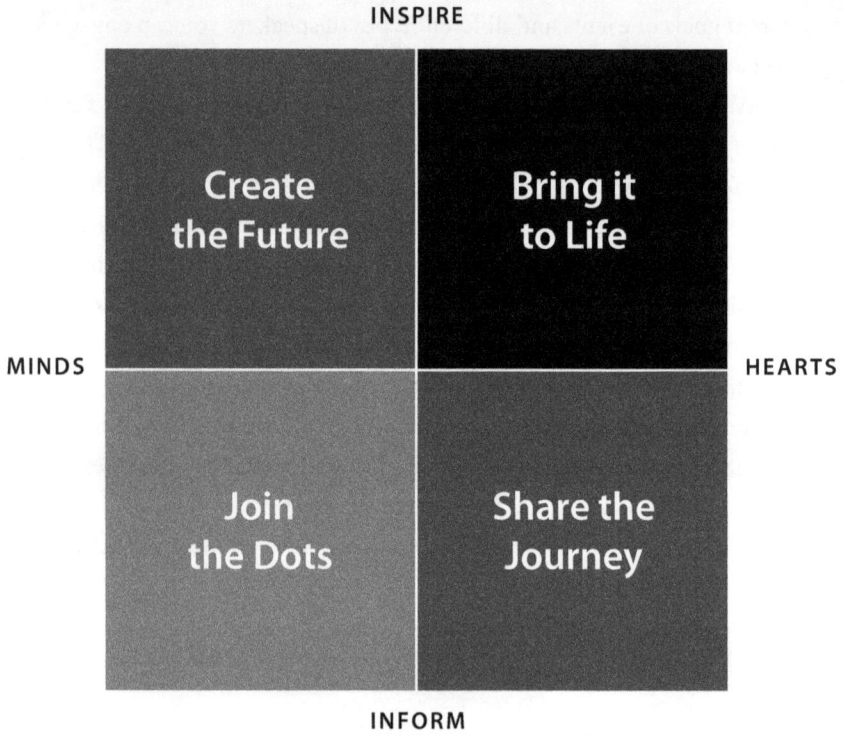

Figure 24. The four speakers at any event

don't work as well as they should. But there are way more than two types of meetings to be had.

The challenge I think is to consider all types of meetings, what they are trying to achieve, and then apply frameworks and guidelines for best practice as they apply to each. In a way, it's like cataloguing personality types in some form of the enneagram, both useful and flawed. The minute you define me as personality A, I will do something that breaks the definition, and you will have to rethink the classification. This is the principle behind statistician George Box's caution that "Essentially, all models are wrong, but some are useful."

In an ideal world your inbox does not run your life, your priorities do. Equally, calendar invites should not plan your day. Project goals should.

We need a useful model for meetings that we can adopt as a guideline, but not a regulation.

I decided to explore some different models that are available, everything from Hippocrates' four body types to some Ayurvedic frameworks, and ended up settling on the ancient Chinese I Ching model. It fits perfectly with the six classic types of meetings and makes it useful to think of planning meetings elementally; earth, fire, air and water and metal and space.

I Ching is one of the oldest books on the planet. Its literal translation is 'The Book of Changes'. I love that name. That's essentially why we meet; to change stuff. We change perceptions, we exchange information, and we change the direction of our pursuits in meetings. Change is the new normal, therefore getting good at meetings—the primary agent of change—is a big idea.

In short, if we know why we are meeting and what we want to achieve, we can make meetings work for us.

Next time you want to call a meeting, consider the six meeting types and apply the guidelines for running them effectively. Often with meetings you will need to mix and combine the six meeting types to achieve your goals but knowing which stage or meeting type you are in is incredibly useful if you wish to make progress through collaboration.

Next time someone asks you to attend a meeting or have a meeting, you may want to get clear on the meeting's intent first. One of my pet peeves is the universal calendar invitation being sent out reflexively without any discussion. The CAL invite is becoming as ubiquitous as email and needs to be defended against as strenuously. In an ideal world your inbox does not run your life, your priorities do. Equally, calendar invites should not plan your day. Project goals should.

The rest of this chapter is an attempt at doing exactly that; classifying and optimising meeting types. The I Ching metaphor is a useful way to remember the most common meeting types and how to make the most out of them (see Figure 25 on page 173).

EARTH

Decision Making

This is the meeting where things get agreed on. They are seen as efficient, one agenda item meetings. Meetings where everyone knows what's being decided and the decision gets made. What are we doing? Who is responsible? When is it happening?

These meetings are quite formal, almost curt in nature and the agenda is adhered to. These meetings are held in meeting rooms. They should be called decision rooms as the only meeting you would ever want to run in one is a DECISION earth-based meeting.

KEY FOCUS

What decision are we making?

KEY TOOL

Reducing choices

ENVIRONMENT

Meeting room — with limited time

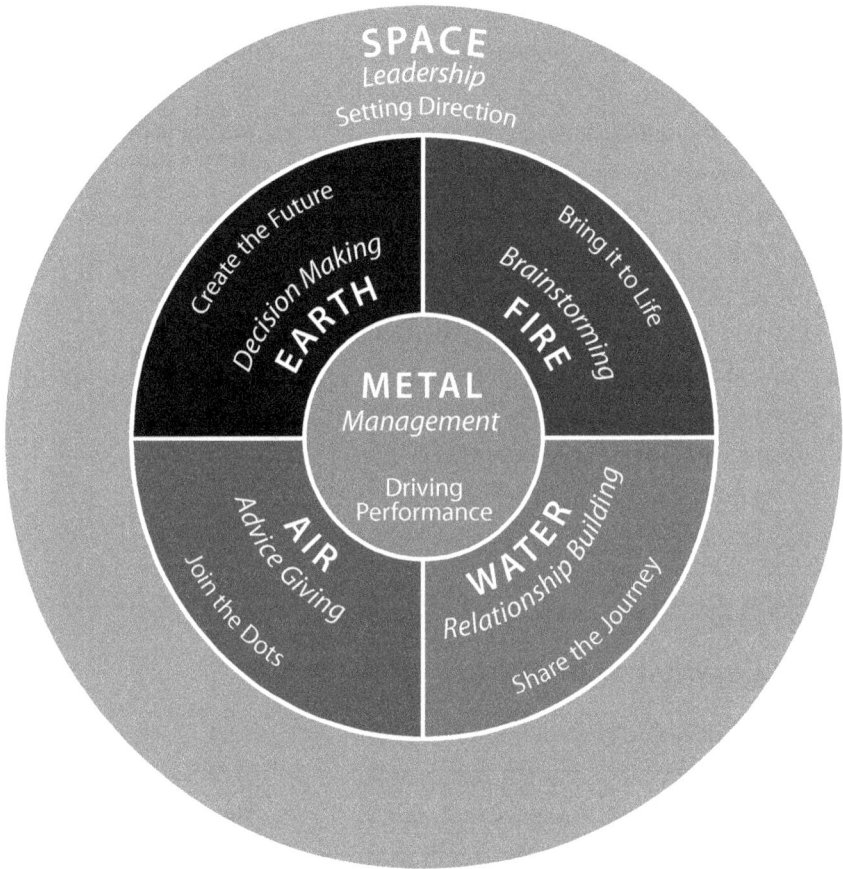

Figure 25. The 6 elemental types of meetings

FIRE

Brainstorming

These creative meetings are held to ideate, to generate more ideas. This is about creativity and expansion. It's about getting beyond the linear and exploring the intersections of exciting ideas.

These meetings need to be fun and non judgemental. They run through stages like IDEATE, COLLABORATE and then AGGREGATE. They're highly visual and are set in comfortable break out environments, generally offsite or off campus.

KEY FOCUS

What else can we think of?

KEY TOOL

Building the right environment

ENVIRONMENT

Offsite in comfortable, flexible space

WATER

Relationship Building

Sometimes you are meeting to extend a relationship. This if often about building a relationship currency with others. These meetings are about opening up paths for conversation and shared understanding. They are a mutual dance of give and take, talk and listen. It's about balance and connection.

A well run networking event should feel like this, although often they are the next meeting type pretending to be about networking.

KEY FOCUS

How can we get to know each other better?

KEY TOOL

Space to share

ENVIRONMENT

Social location, bar, cafe, or restaurant

AIR

Advice Giving

This is the meeting where I pick your brain, shout you a coffee, or quite literally ask you for your advice. This might be in a formal commercial coach/mentor relationship or simply implied by my approach.

These are about relevance and expertise and trying to match the two. Advice sessions should be in a quiet environment. Those giving the advice are respected, those taking the advice are asking questions and documenting the answer. Record what the advisor says.

KEY FOCUS

What would you do in my situation?

KEY TOOL

Respect and learn

ENVIRONMENT

Advisor's favourite place

METAL

Management

This type of meeting is one of accountability. It's about checking in with various parties to make sure they are on track, doing the right thing and have what they need to keep executing.

It's critical that these meetings happen often enough to have a recurring rhythm about them. When they are sprung on people in response to a situation, people will always feel threatened and end up covering their butt instead of making progress.

KEY FOCUS

What do you need to get this done?

KEY TOOL

Cadence and frameworks

ENVIRONMENT

At the team member's desk

Strategy

This is the sixth meeting type, and probably the most important. This is the meeting that plans for the future. Small groups of key decision-makers plan for what's next.

These meetings are not called to cover off the day-to-day or assess whether people are doing their work. These are the ON the business meetings as opposed to the IN the business meetings. This is what boards do (or should).

KEY FOCUS
What is the overarching context to all this?

KEY TOOL
Sense making

ENVIRONMENT
Uninterrupted boardroom key reports/ team members on standby

Once classified, each of these meeting types can have guidelines for optimising them towards their goal. A project update might be served by a 12 minute huddle at noon, but a key relationship would suffer under the constraints of a forced time limit.

Take back your life. Don't let calendar invites and emails rule your world. Turn your meetings from time wasters into agents of change.

ONLINE REFERENCES

1. Seth Godin. 2017. *altMBA*. https://altmba.com

2. Al Pittampali: *"Read This Before Our Next Meeting" | Talks At Google*. https://www.youtube.com/watch?v=Mn-q529ExFw

BOOKS MENTIONED

Pittampalli, A., 2011. *Read This Before Our Next Meeting*. 1st ed. United States: Do You Zoom, Inc.

Wilhelm, R., 1967. *The I Ching, or, Book of Changes* (Bollingen Series XIX) (Bollingen Series (General)). 3rd ed. United States: Princeton University Press.

DISCUSSION IDEAS

1   How big a deal are meetings in your business?

_____

_____

_____

2   How many hours would you spend
at meetings each week?

_____

_____

_____

3   Is there a default time for your meetings?

_____

_____

_____

4   Research Jeff Bezos' Two Pizza Rule and discuss
how that might affect meetings in your business.

_____

_____

_____

5 Review yesterday's meetings in your calendar. Without checking notes what was decided at each meeting? If you don't know, did you need to be there?

_____

_____

_____

6 How can you decline meetings politely?

_____

_____

_____

7 What's the policy around calling meetings in your business?

_____

_____

_____

8 Walk through two of the meeting types with a colleague and discuss how the elemental meeting framework might be rolled out in your business.

_____

_____

_____

LIFE PRODUCTIVE

In the age of robots and outsourcing, we might need to smarten up how we work. Working smarter might mean living smarter. In this chapter I explore the idea that getting things done is as much about your mojo as it is your workflow.

E verything we have learnt about productivity in the 20th century is getting precipitously close to out of date. If we want to become more productive with our work, we need to first understand this context, and then apply ourselves to three new areas of focus. We want productivity tools that are appropriate to the new world, not the old.

1. Process work is getting taken over by robots and AI

All the available evidence is pointing to the death of the middle class process worker. Just as robotic automation has made the blue-collar, assembly line roles of the industrial revolution redundant, artificial intelligence is about to make the information process workers who hold the bulk of white-collar jobs redundant. So much of the world's literature on productivity to date is about processing information more efficiently. But it seems the word 'productivity' itself may need a new definition sooner than we think.

2. Time is the ultimate non-renewable resource

Whatever role each individual fills in the modern workforce, our sheer mortality continues to put pressure on time and the meaningful use of it. The bottom line is, if you choose to work in the future you will most definitely need to work smarter, and with an eye on leveraging every minute you spend at work. We should—nay, must!—be obsessed with getting good things done!

3. Value trumps time

Being at the office, sitting at your desk, simply 'clocking on' doesn't count anymore. The punch card—formerly the sole record of your contribution to the business—is no longer of any relevance in the modern workplace. Too many people engross themselves in 'busyness' every day, yet are generating little value for their clients and employers. Productivity today means solving problems, not counting hours.

There's enormous utility in realising the distinction between time and value. It provides the perspective and motivation to find more efficient, effective, and leveraged ways to work.

Triaging email as your first daily activity may be the single most counterproductive habit with which to start the day, and yet millions of people around the world make it their ritual. It's strangely satisfying, and it feels like work, but pretty much every piece of productivity research concludes it's the worst way to begin your day.

Everything we have learnt about productivity in the 20th century is getting precipitously close to out of date.

The most valuable thing you can do at the start of the day is make the progress you need to on your most important project. But so many people find it much more difficult to reach that milestone or finish that report, when deleting an email is so addictive. Book after book has been written around how you might get more done. Three of the best include: *First Things First* by Dr Stephen Covey, *Getting Things Done* by David Allen and *18 Minutes* by Peter Bregman

A review of these and other productivity texts points to three areas of focus; the first is how efficient you are being, the second is how effective you are being, and the third is how leveraged you are being.

Be efficient

At the most basic level, individual productivity is about efficiency. It's about cranking through your task list and making real progress. Similarly, when you're passing responsibility to someone else, you need them to be functional. An assistant can only assist when they're getting things done. Lots of high-performance people actually slow down when someone comes on board to help them, and generating a functional relationship is key to making progress. In a broader team context, you're aiming for activity. The more people in a team, the more inertia that must be overcome. The first step towards a productive team is a bunch of energised players.

Be effective

As your productivity improves (or your time becomes more constrained), you learn how to do only that which matters. Your effectiveness increases when you only do work which has a lasting impact, and learn to say no to the busywork that fills the average person's day. At this point, you need support that's truly systemised. All your basic requirements are met without any input from you at all. Delegation becomes something you only have to do once, as your assistant/s have a system to deal with every outcome. Teamwork at this level becomes highly strategic. The energy generated to overcome inertia is focused sharply on activities that move the team directly towards your goals.

Be leveraged

As you reach the heights of super productivity, you are getting the most out of every piece of work you do. You work almost exclusively in leverage. Everything you do can be magnified, multiplied, repurposed or reused, so that every minute you spend working creates many hours of value. Your top level support staff are highly engaged. In fact, your assistants are so good you suspect they're

Multi-tasking is a myth and is more accurately called task switching.

better at your job than most of your competitors would be. They're co-pilots, not ground crew. Top level teams are highly aligned, and operate with a fluidity that fosters enormous creativity.

My seven key takeaways for people who want to get things done:

1. Use calendars and lists; don't waste your memory on minutiae

2. Plan your week at the start of the week, and

3. Plan your day the day before

4. Do tough stuff first

5. Don't let other people's stuff dictate your stuff

6. Make work a game

7. Work in bursts

If you're fired up, these habits will help. You'll make progress in your task list and fight the tyranny of overload a little more smartly, but it takes a bit of mojo. You need to 'lean in' and expend energy to make it work. The truth is, all the strategies and tactics in the world won't help you if you don't have the energy for them. Sometimes it's more about the capacity you have in your life around your body, your mind and your soul that will dramatically increase your capacity to work. The nine things in Figure 26 on page 187 won't help you get to inbox zero but they will allow you to get more done. These nine things will lift your overall life-productivity as opposed to simply making your day more productive.

Too many people engross themselves in 'busyness' every day, yet are generating little value for their clients and employers.

The first (bottom) row on this model explore how the body plays a part in helping you get more done. The second explores how your mind is key productivity tool. Finally, the top row gives you a sense of why, a connection to something bigger than you, the soul of your work. Exploring the first column alone is enough to seriously lift your game as a doer.

FITNESS

For most of us, productivity is a mental game, which can lead us to neglect the vehicle that carries our brain around and fuels the thoughts it creates. A base level of physical fitness provides you with more mental energy than almost anything else. Without it you will feel fatigue quicker than you should. It is the first way you can lift your capacity to produce.

	ACTIVITY	PLATFORM	RECHARGE
SOUL	persist **Purpose** *Direction* wander	hope **Belief** *Framework* empty	connect **Beauty** *Integration* isolated
MIND	value **Focus** *Attention* waste	lift **Discipline** *Creation* sabotage	calm **Meditation** *Perspective* chaos
BODY	base **Fitness** *Capacity* fatigue	fuel **Nutrition** *Energy* exhaust	growth **Rest** *Sustainable* decay

**Figure 26. The nine platforms
for a more productive life**

FOCUS

The first idea for developing a mental capacity for work is to manage distractions. Get good at deep focussed work and stop multi-tasking. It turns out multi-tasking is a myth — it is more accurately called task switching. You can only concentrate on one thing at a time. Make it your most important task for the day, your one thing. This means you don't waste any precious mental energy. Focus is essentially about getting the most value out of every minute you have to concentrate.

PURPOSE

The soul level starts with creating a sense of direction or higher purpose to your work. Even if it's 'made up' by you, find some reason to believe that what you are doing matters as part of bigger picture. This helps you persist and finish things, as you don't want to let down the bigger-than-you vision. Without this you wander from idea to idea, starting and never finishing anything, because when the going inevitably gets tough you don't see the point of putting in or sacrificing.

The other six ideas for building your capacity to produce are fairly self-explanatory. Start with the first three ideas and level-up your ability to produce.

Final word

People who can get things done will be highly valued in the future.

People who simply do things will not. Process, management, and status quo supervisors will be out of work.

Working is not an idea for the future, creating is. Go create stuff. Remove the frictions of everyday life and push the edges of what's possible. You being mega productive is a core future-proof skill.

BOOKS MENTIONED

Allen, D., 2001. *Getting Things Done: The Art of Stress-Free Productivity.* 1st ed. United States: Viking Penguin.

Bregman, P., 2011. *18 Minutes: Find Your Focus, Master Distraction, and Get the Right Things Done.* 1st ed. United States: Business Plus.

Covey, S., 1994. *First Things First.* 1st ed. United States: Simon & Schuster.

DISCUSSION IDEAS

1   **What changes might you make to your email habit?**

_____
_____
_____

2   **Read the summaries of the three recommended books.**

_____
_____
_____

3   **Review the Covey Quadrant Model and map out where you spent most of your time yesterday.**

_____
_____
_____

4   **Look at the different situational contexts in _Getting Things Done_ and break todays task list into situational contexts.**

_____
_____
_____

5 Start a learning journal dedicated to being productive.

---

6 Pick one of the nine integrations to work on this month.

---

7 Review the seven takeaways list and have
a group discussion about each tip.

THE FEROCIOUS FIVE

Often the best work happens when you lose yourself in the intense concentration of an absorbing task. There are a lot of distractions though, so getting clear and intentional about your priorities is key. This chapter focuses on that intense small set of tasks that, if we get them done, makes almost everything else become unnecessary or redundant.

t's a well-known idea that 80% of your results will come from 20% of your effort. Similarly, 20% of your clients will contribute to 80% of your sales.

The 80/20 principle has been published in many forms, including a book of that exact title by Richard Koch. The 80/20 rule was derived from the observations of 19th Century Italian economist Vilfredo Pareto, who famously noted that 80% of the land in Italy was held by 20% of the families. Pareto expanded this principle across to other countries and noted that the same rule was roughly followed everywhere and applied to the distribution of power, income, and wealth. James Clear has written a brilliant bio on the Pareto narrative.[1]

Today this ratio is often used to explain the difference between the 'Haves' and the 'Have Nots'. It defines the difference between being efficient (someone who is across everything) and effective (someone who focuses on the right thing) and is used in account management to differentiate Category A, B and C clients. The same segmentation principle is the key to managing high levels of service or advice to a small number of people, and prioritising the effective 20% above everything else.

There is always a single piece of work each day that has to be done.

In the book *The One Thing*, Gary Keller asks a basic yet clarifying question: "What is the one thing that if you did it today, would make doing everything else redundant or unnecessary?" Aligned with this ruthless focus, modern productivity practices support the idea that there is always a single piece of work each day that has to be done. So what if you did that first, and didn't attempt anything else until it was done? Would you need to do the other stuff?

I believe I can process 20 tasks a day. If I'm ferocious about one task each day, this 5% will have the greatest leverage.

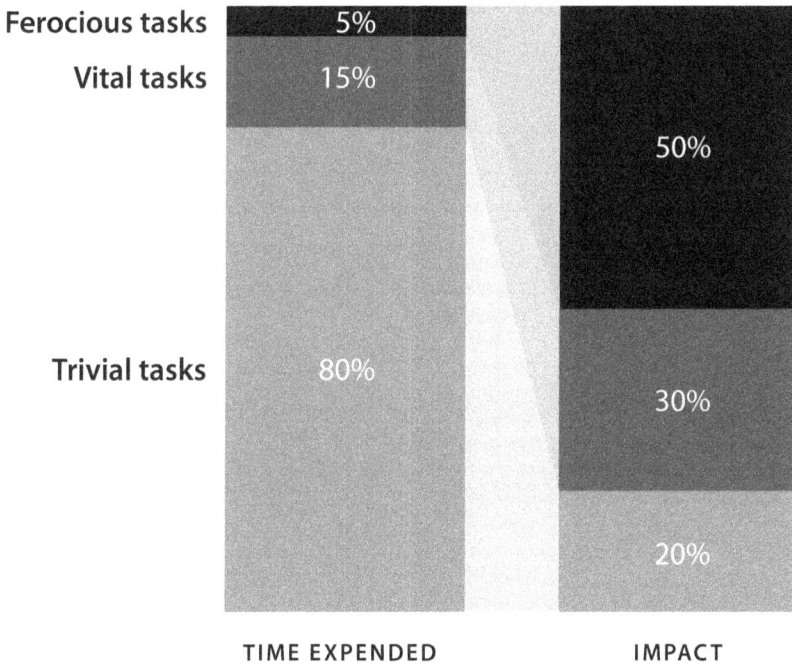

Figure 27.   Time versus impact

I challenge you to find out what your one thing is each day, and at the same time get clear on the five things which you do that no one else can. In my world it's Thinking, Writing, Presenting, Aligning value and Mentoring. I can run a team meeting (not sure I should); I can review the finances (not sure I could); I can fill out a form (not sure I would). Of course, this doesn't mean that team meetings, spreadsheets, and signing documents don't get done. Just not always by me.

In a normal life, there are tasks that must get done due to responsibilities or because you haven't put those tasks into a system or procedure where they're completed by someone else. It may be washing your car, cooking your meals, cleaning your house, booking your travel, paying bills. Doing the ordinary tasks is fine — until they stop you from doing the extraordinary stuff.

Extraordinary results require a ferocious commitment to the few things that only you can do. Does a surgeon order gauze, clean instruments, or administer anaesthetic?

Athletes and adventurers are some of the most selfish people on the planet. They've needed to be, to reach the heights that they have.

Maybe you need to give yourself permission to rewrite the rules of expectation and redefine what exactly your work is. As more and more tasks are outsourced (to cheaper labour), automated (to systems and software), or possessed (taken over by deep learning networks), I think we need more focus on what our purpose should be. Attack the 5% as a priority, and explore where that can take us.

Is it arrogant, indulgent or selfish to outsource the normal? I'd say YES! But it's also essential to find out what we're capable of. Athletes and adventurers are some of the most selfish people on the planet. They've needed to be, to reach the heights that they have. The reason the Renaissance period is famously filled with masterpieces is that the Medici family provided many artists with their food, clothing, shelter, and materials. This allowed the artists to focus on what they did best and paint chapels, sculpt marble, and carve statues.

George Bernard Shaw said it best when he stated:

> "The reasonable man adapts himself to the world; the unreasonable one persists in trying to adapt the world to himself. Therefore all progress depends on the unreasonable man."

Sometimes I choose to wash my car. My son joins me, my dog chases the hose, and I get some sun on my back. And sometimes I pay someone else to wash the car, so I can do something else with my time. It's not about being better than a task at hand. It is about being intentional.

Live a life by design, not default. Find the path travelled best by you and walk that often. Establish what you do that others can't, won't, or don't; and spend more time in that space.

Be focused on the 20% and then be ferocious about the 5%.

ONLINE REFERENCES

1. James Clear. 2017. *The 1 Percent Rule: Why a Few People Get Most of the Rewards.* http://jamesclear.com/the-1-percent-rule

BOOKS MENTIONED

Keller, G., 2013. *The ONE Thing: The Surprisingly Simple Truth Behind Extraordinary Result.* 1st ed. United States: Bard Press.

Koch, R., 1998. *The 80/20 Principle: The Secret of Achieving More with Less.* 1st ed. United States: Currency Books / Doubleday & Company, Inc..

DISCUSSION IDEAS

1 List out the 10 big tasks you have to do today.

_____

_____

_____

2 Which one of these is the most important one?

_____

_____

_____

3 What if you only did that today?

_____

_____

_____

4 What stops you doing that first today?

_____

_____

_____

5 If you did not have to work, what tasks
would you pay attention to most?

_____

_____

_____

6 If you did not have to work, what would
you definitely not keep doing?

_____

_____

_____

7 What activity do you need to let go of so that
you free yourself up to do something better?

_____

_____

_____

ORDER v CHAOS

Maybe discipline and organisation are overrated. This chapter is designed with the intent to start a conversation around how different people work. Its aim is to deal with the phrase 'work smarter not harder', but to do so through the central idea that what works for you is the smartest way of working.

have a confession to make. I came up with the ideas in this chapter when I realised that most time management/personal effectiveness programs I attended made me feel lazy and useless.

I have a history of nodding along at these programs, all the while knowing that something was fundamentally amiss. I wasn't going to block out two hours on a Monday to plan my week. I wasn't going to make a meeting with myself every Friday to run through roles, goals, and priorities. I wasn't going to feel inspired to work if I cleared my desk.

I have tried doing these things, bought a new pencil case, got excited and then, well, I simply don't do more. Clean desks are not always important to me. Meetings with myself feel like prison. And while the Inbox Zero,[1] *Getting Things Done* conversation made sense, and the idea of the order it created was seductive, I found it was not always useful.

Maybe order isn't always a good thing?

The problem is most personal effectiveness programs are designed by disciplined, organised people in an attempt to get the rest of us to do what they do. This isn't always an effective strategy; one person's 'smart' may be another person's 'dumb'. Or more accurately it might be smarter from time to time to ignore these methodical processes. When work flows shift from order to chaos, you don't have to feel like you have fallen off the productivity wagon. Maybe you have jumped on the creativity express!

A journalist interviewing the late, great Luciano Pavarotti once remarked on his body of work and said he must be highly disciplined to have achieved so much. Pavarotti looked down at his expanding waistline and said "I think you mistake obsession for discipline!" Pavarotti got lots done, but was not at all disciplined. He was determined, he was passionate — obsessed even — but not disciplined.

This chapter is an invitation to see getting things done as requiring something more than will power, a methodical approach, and a well-maintained day planner. Maybe some of the things you need to get done come from a chaotic, creative, passionately-obsessed space, not a well-ordered, calmly-executed, inbox-zero space.

I consider myself incredibly productive. I definitely get things done. But I don't get them done because they are written on a list (even if I write lists sometimes). I don't get them done because I have blocked out two hours on a Tuesday (although I might block out Tuesday completely to focus on one thing). I don't get them done because of some fabulous context-managing, cloud-based software (even though I do use Apple's Reminders[2] and the task app Things[3]).

I get things done because I 'follow the energy' in projects and have learnt to hack my own preferences and priorities. The trick is to know your personal productivity platform preference and then learn how to switch it on and off at will.

Central to this idea is a stand against the typical productivity gurus and the negative impact that their process can have on creative knowledge work. Processing

The problem is, most personal effectiveness programs are designed by disciplined, organised people in an attempt to get the rest of us to do what they do.

inputs daily, like a machine, is quite different to locking yourself up for three days in a chaotic, immersed 'do fest', where you'll likely be creating magic (albeit running the risk of cutting off an ear in the process). You might get more good work done if you stop trying to do all your work and start creating magic.

So if normal productivity tools don't work for you all the time, read on. You might find solace and comfort in the ideas that follow. The process? First discover your own personal productivity platform (chaos versus order) then use this awareness to increase your personal effectiveness. Work smarter not harder.

Your personal productivity platform

The model in Figure 28 on page 204 contrasts people with low discipline and high discipline, and those with a narrow focus and a wide focus. Knowing where you are positioned on this model—whether because it's your personality type, or simply how you feel that day or week or year—allows you to identify the steps you need to take to get to where you want to be. I acknowledge that the boundaries between the two main categories are blurred, and that attempts to categorise people can be overly simplistic. The main objective is not to label who you are, but to make the most of where you're at on any given project at any given moment.

LOWER LEFT

Dumb

We all have times when we are not very productive: those moments of 'dumbness' are a part of life. Knowing when you are in a productivity funk is one of the smartest things you can do. For some people this can happen daily, weekly, monthly or yearly.

You might get more good work done if you stop trying to do all your work and start creating magic.

Without gainful employment for a few months it is easy to get into a rut and not work at your 'smartest'. Without a reason to do good work, it is easy to slide into a routine of clocking on then clocking off, having achieved basically nothing. The 'dumb' quadrant does not describe you, but rather acknowledges that you are not doing your best at the moment, regardless of your personal platform.

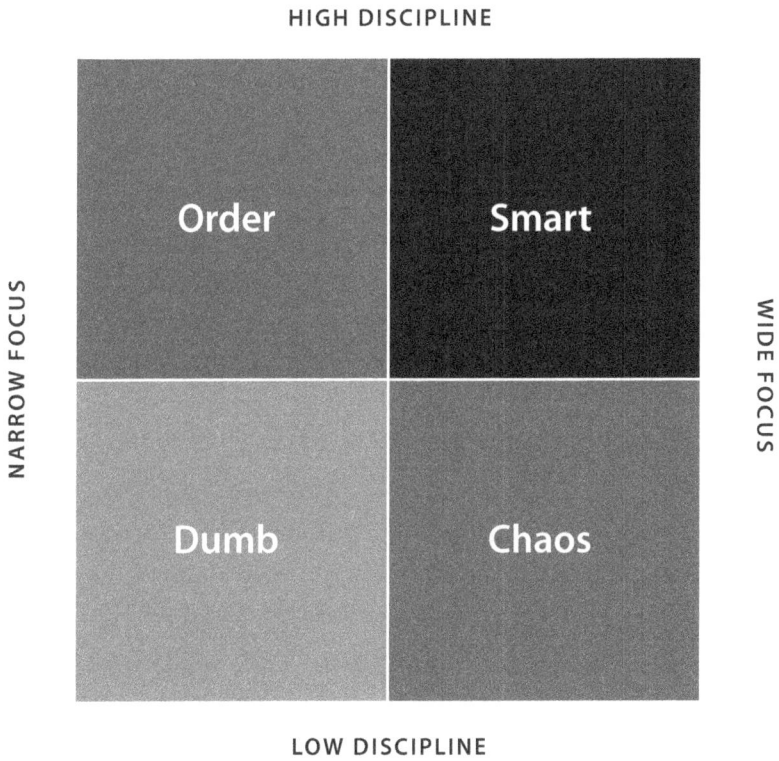

Figure 28. The four work platforms

Order

The second quadrant is the domain of the dedicated thinker, who uses order to get things done: highly disciplined, committed, reliable, and on time. These people manage the detail of their lives brilliantly. They know the exact number of words required for the annual report, when it is due, and the format required. They read emails in detail and carefully consider their response before they reply.

Indications that you prefer to work in the Order quadrant:

- Your emails are often thorough and contain more than one action item within it. 'Send it once and make it complete' is your mantra.

- You read one book at a time and only read when you have the time or the right head-space. Holiday reading is often your catch up time.

- You can't stand channel surfing — you pick one TV show to watch and settle in a chair five minutes before it starts with a drink and snack ready to go.

- If a report is due in on Monday at 10am, you have it 80% complete on Friday with the final tweaks added in a fresh head space an hour before it's due.

- You find it hard to return to deep thought after an interruption.

LOWER RIGHT

Chaos

Sometimes your work flows from a state of chaos; never switching off, mulling over ideas and procrastinating. It's like you are thinking continuously. When working with chaos your inbox can drive your day (a bad idea for both order and chaos workflows), especially if you feel guilty about not having achieved inbox zero. The goal of zero emails in your inbox is a factory mindset, not the mindset of an artists. Artists may need to ignore an email from someone for a day or so until they achieve clarity.

The problem is some of the things you work on need to be absorbed, slept on, bounced off others and put down and picked up several times. Staring at the problem for exactly 30 minutes at 11am on Tuesday probably won't get the best outcome. When working in a chaos state, a long email from a methodical person with many requests for clarity is hard to process. So you, the 'chaos' worker, respond by answering the easiest or most important question and ignoring the rest. When working in the chaos quadrant you are easily distracted and often go walkabout. You might have several books on the go at one time and often don't complete them because you get bored or are doing something else.

Knowing where you are positioned on this model allows you to identify the steps you need to take to get to where you want to be.

Indications that you prefer working in the chaos quadrant:

- You hate arbitrary deadlines, yet paradoxically your best work happens in the final moments before a project is due. Other people often think you're straining under pressure at the last minute, because you lack the discipline to work through your project in stages.

- You seem to do nothing for days, then all of a sudden have a productivity blitz and deliver high-value work that sets new standards.

- You watch three TV shows at once, flicking through the channels hoping to find the most entertaining one at that minute. And half the time you'll be watching your phone or tablet at the same time.

- You rarely switch off. You are always thinking, although you might not be aware of it.

- You know that by taking a walk, 'sleeping on it', or going to a movie, your creative wash cycle might just 'figure it out'.

UPPER RIGHT

Working Smarter

This final quadrant is the sweet spot for all of us.

It's the 'Smart ' quadrant — the one where both workflows come together and achieve amazing things. Those who prefer to work in the Chaos quadrant become finishers and dependable and those most comfortable in the Order quadrant are able to let things that don't matter slide and stay on the critical path.

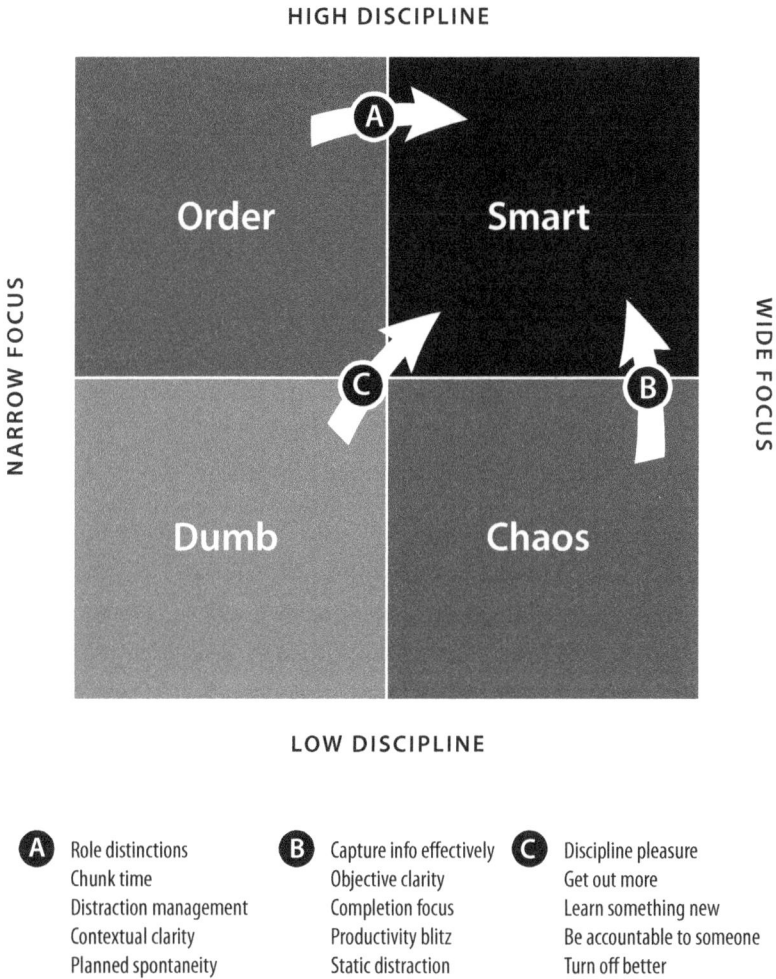

HIGH DISCIPLINE

Order

Smart

NARROW FOCUS

WIDE FOCUS

Dumb

Chaos

LOW DISCIPLINE

A Role distinctions
Chunk time
Distraction management
Contextual clarity
Planned spontaneity

B Capture info effectively
Objective clarity
Completion focus
Productivity blitz
Static distraction

C Discipline pleasure
Get out more
Learn something new
Be accountable to someone
Turn off better

Figure 29.   Moving towards working smarter

Action Items — How to move quadrants

A **FIVE IDEAS THAT HELP THOSE WHO PREFER ORDER TO WORK SMARTER**

Role Distinctions
Be familiar with the different hats you wear and your role when wearing each hat. Don't blend your roles.

Chunk time
Plan your days in blocks of time and stop what you're doing when time is up. Discipline yourself to do the tasks in the time allocated, and accept that you won't get everything finished.

Distraction management
Learn to say "No" and have some 'conversational scripts' on hand to stop people interrupting you. In an open plan office try to do something that signals 'do not interrupt me', such as wearing headphones that may not even be plugged into anything!

Contextual clarity
Always keep an eye on the big picture. Ask yourself, "Is this the best use of my time?" Track the critical path of each project and do the big tasks first.

Planned spontaneity
Dedicate chunks of time in your day to unplanned activity. Use this for both your business and personal life. Embrace the messiness of creative pursuits.

B FIVE IDEAS THAT HELP THOSE WHO PREFER CHAOS TO WORK SMARTER

Capture information more effectively
Have dedicated journals for all your notes and avoid loose bits of paper. For example, have one for ideas and one for meetings.

Objective clarity
Focus on the outcome of the meeting or project. Ask the questions "What do we need to achieve here today?" and "What question are we asking?

Completion focus
Spend your time getting things to the next stage rather than starting new projects. Consider a project list where you simply list all your current projects and dates for when you want them completed. Become aware of sequence and advance each project like the 'pucks' on a shuffleboard game.

Productivity blitz
Immerse yourself totally in an activity and don't stop until it's done — a continuous single-minded focus. "Today I clean my desk." or "This afternoon I prepare that presentation."

Static distraction
Use noise and crowded places as a way of focusing on a task. Non-specific noise helps a chaos person do more.

C FIVE IDEAS THAT HELP ALL OF US WHEN WE HAVE DROPPED OUT OF THE 'MAKING STUFF HAPPEN' GAME

The hardest quadrant to move out of is the lower left, as we have to shift both our focus and discipline. This 'Dumb' quadrant is a place that we all visit when we hit a funk. We are less smart about our time or work, often becoming trapped in patterns of behaviour.

Discipline pleasure

Start setting little rules around what you do in your downtime, e.g., there is no TV or a shower until you have done some sit ups.

Get out more

New perspectives help you break out of your rut by giving you the inspiration to shift back into your preferred mode of either Order or Chaos. Remember, we need to do this before we can move up to working Smarter.

Learn something new

Learning something new is a simple way to rapidly get out of a 'doing' rut.

Be accountable to someone

Declare a goal to a friend, coach or boss to help you follow through on your commitment. There's nothing quite like peer pressure and living in integrity. Put signs and targets on your wall such as 'Exercise every day for the next ten days.'

Turn off better

When we are in a rut we numb out and are happy to wind down with whatever is at hand. Try recording the TV shows you want to watch, rather than channel surfing and watching rubbish.

Don't make yourself wrong in the game of getting things done, make yourself strong. Figure out how work works for you and work that way, not the way imposed by others. You just might be amazed how much you create when you increase your productivity IQ.

ONLINE REFERENCES

1. Merlin Mann. 2017. *43 Folders Series: Inbox Zero.* http://www.43folders.com/izero

2. How-To Geek. 2015. *How to Use the Reminders App on Your Mac or iPhone and Never Forget Something Again.* http://www.howtogeek.com/236278/how-to-use-the-reminders-app-on-your-mac-or-iphone-and-never-forget-something-again.

3. Wired. 2017. *'Things' Might Be The Prettiest To-Do List App Ever.* https://www.wired.com/2017/05/things-might-prettiest-list-app-ever

BOOKS MENTIONED

Allen, D., 2001. *Getting Things Done: The Art of Stress-Free Productivity.* 1st ed. United States: Viking Penguin.

DISCUSSION IDEAS

1 Which quadrant do you spend most of your time in?

_____

_____

_____

2 Looking at the list of actions that move you towards Smart, find another like-minded person and deep dive on the strategies suggested.

_____

_____

_____

3 Write out the five actions that are most helpful to you and place them front of mind in your diary, wallet, or screen at work.

_____

_____

_____

4 Sit with someone who is the opposite to
you and ask them three questions:

i What about how I work frustrates you the most?

_____

_____

_____

ii What one thing do you need from me to
make working together more effective?

_____

_____

_____

iii How does understanding my work style
help you work better with me?

_____

_____

_____

SPEAK MORE BETTERER

Speakership—the art of oration and the science of influence—is the new leadership imperative. Whether you want to increase your leadership credentials to grow your career, build your communication skills as the head of your business to motivate staff and compel your clients, or deliver keynotes from stage to make public speaking your profession, this chapter was written for you.

Becoming a confident and compelling speaker might be the most important influence skill for leaders in business. James C. Humes, US Presidential speechwriter, said it brilliantly "Speakership is leadership. Every time you speak in public, you are auditioning for a leadership position." Speak better in public and see leadership results improve.

It puzzles me that more people don't commit more effort to becoming great public speakers. Becoming a confident and compelling speaker might be the most important skill for leaders in the modern business landscape. I've dedicated two decades to speaking professionally, teaching others the craft, and collecting and creating speaking resources. For someone with a lot of ideas and projects on the go, I'm pretty single-minded about speaking with impact. You should be too!

Speakership is the missing link between strategy and execution, between wanting to have people do something and inspiring them to take action.

Too many people with so much to offer flirt with the idea of spreading ideas through powerful speaking, and then are overcome with the enormity of the task. Daunted by the lift that is required to get good at leadership speaking.

Communication has become one of the most puzzling paradoxes of our time. We live in a world that is hyper-connected; more plugged in, tuned in, turned on than ever before. Everything we need to know is just a swipe away on a mobile device the size of your hand that has more computing power than NASA used to put two men on the moon in 1969! Want to know the temperature in Brazil right now? The price of corn in Maine? How about finding an old friend from high school? Most likely they are just a google search away. The world has irrevocably shrunk.

And yet, social scientists tell us that more and more people feel isolated and disconnected from their communities. They feel overworked, underpaid, misunderstood, and alone. Despite the capability to be 'in touch' twenty four hours a day, seven days a week, many people are disengaged and disillusioned. Business leaders know the struggle to engage and empower a workforce that clocks in, then checks out.

Speakership is the key to inspiring teams to seize new opportunities, and motivate people through change and disruption. Use it well and you will show confidence as a leader, increase collaboration amongst your teams and ultimately become the personal catalyst that kickstarts progress on those big change initiatives.

When your best people lead out loud, you can stake a claim to territory in the market and build a reputation as thought leaders.

When your best people lead out loud, you can stake a claim to territory in the market and build a reputation as thought leaders. Ultimately, you can shift from a business to a brand by becoming an integral part of the cultural landscape. It enables your people to achieve success on the triple bottom line; commercially, professionally, and socially.

A leader creates clarity from confusion, turns fear into confidence and mobilises people to act in pursuit of a better future. You can't lead your team into battle with an underwhelming whisper.

Those who can articulate the way forward, who inspire with powerful messages, who motivate and provide clarity and make meaning when they speak; these will be the leaders of the near future. Your ability to step up and cut through the noise of mass media, to provoke new insights, to challenge the status quo and bring every group you speak to closer to the central vision of your organisation is what will set you apart. It's a lot to do with your centre of attention.

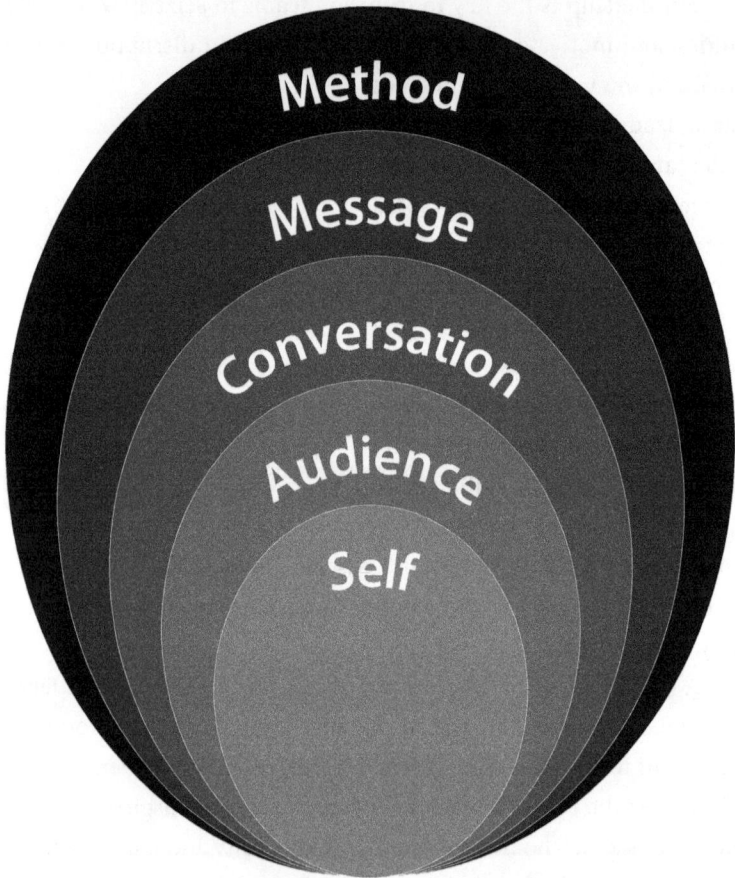

Figure 30.   The five rings of attention
when you speak in public

RING 1

Self

When you focus on 'you' when you speak, you are bound to get undone. In your head, everything becomes an 'I' issue. 'I' am not prepared; 'I' am not qualified; 'I' am not wearing clothes that make me comfortable. First step; you need to get over yourself. At this ring, you should quickly coach yourself and replace the negative self-focus with the question of "What can you offer that might be of service to the room?"

RING 2

Audience

Most of the advice you get on how to handle nerves comes from this centre of attention. Well-meaning bad advice, such as 'picture your audience naked' and 'stare at their foreheads', is simply not helpful. That's an acceptable strategy if you are planning to speak once in your life for 15 minutes, but it's not okay if you are committed to being a world-class presenter.

RING 3

Conversation

This ring is the first of the elevating rings. The three elevating outer rings of Conversation, Message, and Method all work together to help you truly manage your internal state and keep an appropriate level of focus, without becoming overwhelmed by the experience. The Conversation ring is about getting into dialogue with the audience. I often use rhetorical questions with very large audiences to give an appearance of a two-way conversation, but of course, only I am speaking.

RING 4

Message

You have to have something to say worth listening to. That seems obvious, right? It is amazing, though, how often we are okay saying something that is obvious, already understood, and easily read or reviewed outside of the live audience experience. When preparing a message for the live audience, you need to spend more time on the words, the key ideas, and how you can use repetitive variety to bring the thoughts out of your mind and pass it to theirs.

RING 5

Method

Start to think about how you say what you are saying. Develop a third-eye perspective through which you begin to watch the science and art of oration. The trick is to stay engaged and connected to what is happening in the room and to have a range of techniques you can use to change the direction, energy and feeling in the room.

When you are controlling your internal dialogue, aware of the needs of your audience, engaged in the conversation with the room, and delivering a message that they value in a way that is compelling, there is simply no time to get nervous. If you start from the outer rings and work back through rings 5–4–3, and then 2 and 1 take care of themselves.

As I write this, the most popular TED talk of all time—Sir Ken Robinson's treatise on schools killing creativity in children[1]—has been viewed almost 44 million times, and not always just by a single person at their PC. It's been shown in groups, classrooms, conferences and more. Consider the impact that twenty minute presentation has had around the globe.

Think of the number of lives that will be different (and better) as a result of that meme being powerfully shared with educators the world over. This is a shining example of speakership. If the only thing Sir Ken did in his life was deliver that speech, he would have had more impact on the world than 99% of all people that have ever lived.

A leader creates clarity from confusion, turns fear into confidence, and mobilises people to act in pursuit of a better future.

Now, more than ever, we need inspired leaders who inspire us. Challenging leaders who challenge us. Now, more than ever, speakership is leadership.

In business and in life, mastery of speakership creates opportunity and impact. Those willing to invest the time and effort into developing their speakership skills will inevitability find themselves with more opportunities, more invitations, and the growing confidence to take those opportunities in both hands. There isn't a personal development program in the world that will accelerate your leadership growth more than committing to standing on a stage, or at the front of the meeting room, and auditioning to lead. Speakership is leadership, and every tribe needs a leader. Will it be you?

ONLINE REFERENCES

1. TED. 2006. Ken Robinson: *Do schools kill creativity?*
   https://www.ted.com/talks/ken_robinson_says_schools_kill_creativity

DISCUSSION IDEAS

1 **What could you talk about that is aligned, yet apart, from your products or services?**

_____

_____

_____

2 **Where do your ideal clients hang out, where could you speak that message?**

_____

_____

_____

3 **What internal events could you speak at to influence the business agenda with more impact?**

_____

_____

_____

4 **What stops you being a better public speaker?**

_____

_____

_____

5 What do you think has the most impact:
a one-on-one conversation, an email, or
a speech at a company offsite?

_____

_____

_____

6 What topics should you save for one-
on-one conversations?

_____

_____

_____

7 What topics are better delivered to a group of
people as opposed to one-on-one conversations?

_____

_____

_____

LISTENING TO LEAD

There is a lot you can achieve by asking the right questions. Leaders-as-coach has been on the landscape for years. The idea is a response to the flattening of organisations and the need to drive a decentralised leadership throughout the business. Stop telling them what to do, and help them discover what needs to be done instead. It's a bit like doing kid's projects for them; no one really benefits. This chapter explores some different ways you can listen to lead.

have the auditory equivalence of a photographic memory. I remember pretty much everything that people say to me. Imagine living with that — poor Lexie!

As a result, I have to be quite selective about what I choose to listen to and the level of conversation and depth I have in my day-to-day life.

I slept very little as a child, because I would replay conversations in my head, searching for meaning and insights. Seeing the world through these filters means that at times I speak when I should listen and at others times I listen when I should have spoken up.

Listening is pretty poorly done across all fields, and the advice on listening is fairly lightweight.

Listening is pretty poorly done across all fields, and the advice on listening is fairly light weight. One of my pet peeves is the proselytising of Active listening, a process wherein I engage in repeating your last word in a sentence and deliver that word with a tone of enquiry.

— Enquiry? Yeh, you know, an upwards inflection to create the illusion of a question.

— Question? Yeh, like I said, it's a process designed to make me do the talking.

— Mmm Talking? Yeh, sharing my opinion in words, sound, wind, vocal chords, etc.

— Mmm Etc?

I'm not a big fan of that.

I think that leaders who listen well realise it's so much more than simply active and passive listening. Let's call it deep listening: not just listening to what someone says, but leading through listening.

For the last decade or more, leader-as-coach has been advanced as a leadership capability. Leader-as-coach has increased empowerment and driven higher engagement and productivity in business. This has been a necessary part of the shift from command-and-control 'Tell' leadership styles to a more empowered flattening of organisations designed to drive ownership and engagement. It might be time to take that skill, the art of listening, a little deeper. Time to explore how we can listen to create an effect.

There's a great interview of entrepreneur Bill Liao[1] which explores some crazy ideas on listening.

It got me thinking around the fact that we might actually have many different types of listening. The breakdown between Passive listening, wherein I am actually waiting for my turn to talk, and Active listening, the rabbiting effect mentioned above, may not be the most useful way to look at listening. Passive and Active listening essentially deal only with turn-taking, with making sure that you give the other person adequate time to communicate their thoughts. But this makes no reference to the purpose of your listening. It doesn't allow for the intention of getting a specific outcome from the conversation.

Passive and Active listening … doesn't allow for the intention of getting a specific outcome from the conversation.

This chapter explores different listening approaches. I hope it's a conversation starter.

The model begins with a North, South, East, West framework (see Figure 31 on page 230).

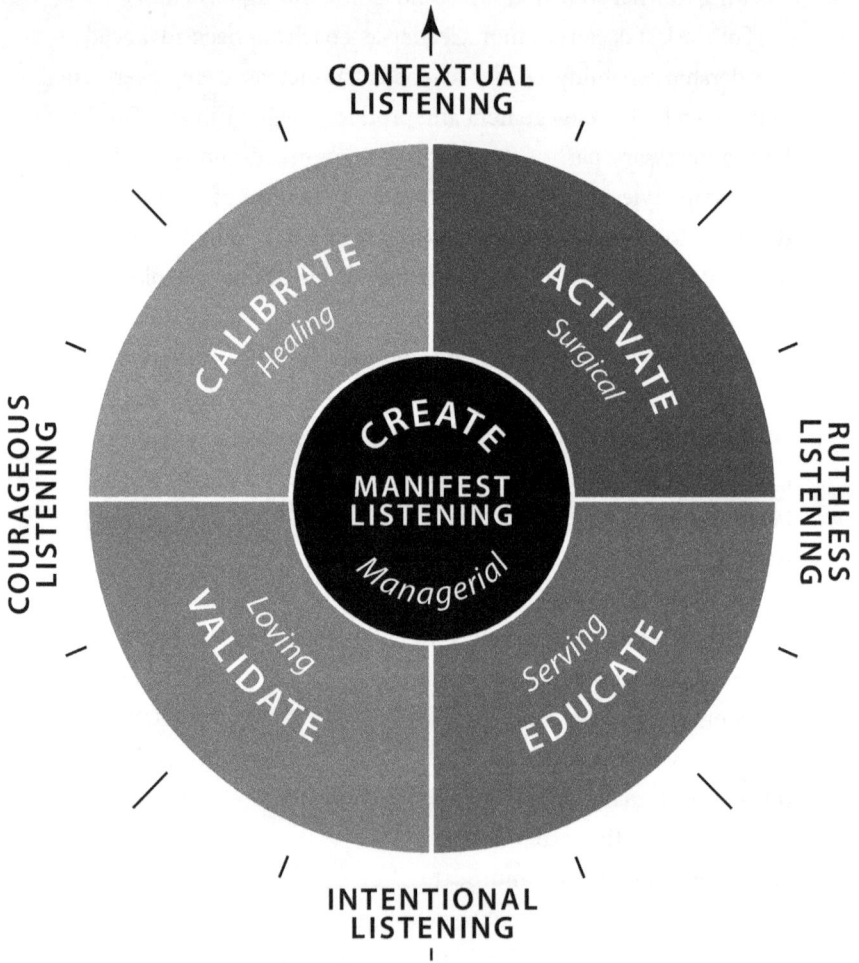

Figure 31.   Listening to Lead

NORTH

Contextual listening

This is a detached form of listening. It's about listening above the stuff. The intent is searching for patterns and it's about asking the question 'What's this really about?'

This echoes the science of pattern recognition and mosaic thinking.

SOUTH

Intentional listening

This is an empathic form of listening. It's about experiencing deeply the world of another. It has a deeply compassionate intent — 'I am them' — asking the question "If I put myself in their shoes, how does that feel?"

This echoes the Buddhist idea of interbeing.

For a great explanation of how to do intentional listening, have a look at the video by John Wineland and Guru Jagat.[2] They walk through an intentional dialogue, and explain why it is so important to develop this skill.

EAST

Ruthless Listening

This is a very directed form of listening and possibly the most dangerous. It's about sorting through what someone says with a pre-determined filter firmly in place. It's about finding informaation to back up a hypothesis. It has the intent of 'looking for evidence' and asks the question "What's really going on here?"

This echoes the forensic nature of a detective with a theory searching for evidence.

Courageous Listening

Possibly the hardest type of listening there is, this about the listener considering that they may be wrong. It's about the listener dropping internal walls and lowering their defences. It must be bold, as it questions the very heart of the listener's self image. It has an intent of 'you may be right' and answers the question "What if what I know to be true, is not?"

This echoes the idea of 360 degree feedback and conscious/unconscious competence.

Manifest Listening.

Certainly the oddest of the listening types. And a bit 'woo hoo', so ignore this one if you are biased to science. If, however, you have a little attention on the ontological conversation then consider this: Bill Lao's video suggests that there is a chance to affect, through your listening, the state of the person you are listening to. Crazy idea, unless it makes sense to you. I decided to put it on the model as it fits logically, even if the idea is not.

Deep listening has the potential to delight in the unknown and introduce new insights.

Deep Listening

This is like a magnetic field and is the combination of all these listening types and more. While the five core listening types are purposeful, like heading out in an adventure to discover something specific, deep listening is about exploring. It's bigger and has less boundaries. It has the potential to delight in the unknown and introduce new insights. Oliver Wendell Holmes once said "The mind once stretched by a new idea never regains its original dimensional." Deep listening bends the mind. Oscar Trimboli, one of the country's leading thinkers in this topic and a brilliant leadership coach, says:

> "Listening as an act of discovery helps you focus on the process, the content and the other person. With an intention of exploration, the impact is wider and deeper. It creates new spaces for insight and learning for you and for them."

I recommend reading Oscar Trimboli's book, *Deep Listening*, on understanding listening as an exploration of possibility rather than a discovery of a predetermined intent.

In the intersections of the various types of listening are our intents, our goals if you like. These four quadrants and the centre help you achieve a leadership outcome by turning up one or the other boundary compass points. Listening to lead is an intuitive process of adapting to three forces: what is said, how it's being said, and what you — as the leader — determine needs to be achieved. Don't just listen, listen deeply.

Activate

If your intent is to activate something in the person you are leading then be surgical and look for what is blocking or causing a resistance to change. Do this well and the conversation becomes transformative.

Educate

If your intent is to educate then listen for gaps in knowledge and serve the person you are leading by giving them the right information at the right moment in the right way. Do this well and you develop a role as mentor/advisor, building the capabilities of those you lead.

Validate

If you are aware that what is required is some strong personal validation then be relational, understanding the other person and expressing what you love about who they are and what they do. Do this well and the people you lead are respected, loyal and genuinely connected to your best interests.

Calibrate

If your goal is to calibrate the relationship and get it back on course then approach the listening with a healing approach. If done well there should be a complete reformation in how you work with the person you are leading.

Create

If you have a custodial goal around holding a space for a bigger future or helping create the best version of someone, then your approach should be 'listening to potentiality' Ask the question "How can we create a new reality in this discussion?" This echoes the idea of leading the witness in legal fields, in so far as you have a clue as to where the conversation could go, and the ontological work of many self-help gurus, in that you are holding the space as a listener to manifest something.

The bottom line is, if you want your conversations to be as effective and meaningful as possible, make your listening intentional. Go into the conversation knowing which type of listening you're doing, and move around the framework as necessary.

ONLINE REFERENCES

1. Bill Lao. *Entrepreneur Bill Liao on the importance of listening.* https://www.youtube.com/watch?v=ImHfNmA9F0s

2. John Wineland and Guru Jagat. *Intentional Dialogue with John Wineland and Guru Jagat.* https://www.youtube.com/watch?v=S9VY5oM8s6Y

BOOKS MENTIONED

Trimboli, O., 2017. *Deep Listening: Impact beyond words.* 1st ed. Australia: Amazon Digital Services LLC.

DISCUSSION IDEAS

1 Have you explored leader-as-coach programs in your current role?

_____
_____
_____

2 What do you think the benefit of listening is over telling?

_____
_____
_____

3 Why don't we listen to others as well as we should?

_____
_____
_____

4 Explore each of the listening styles in the model. Which one feels more natural than the others?

_____
_____
_____

5 Is there one style you reckon would be very difficult for you to use straight away?

_____

_____

_____

FEEDFORWARD

Not all feedback is good, constructive or useful. Take control and be strategic about who you listen to and what advice you take on board. Taking feedback is an active, strategic game, not a passive, reactive game. How easy is it to think that all advice is good advice? That you should listen to everything that anyone has to say to you. That a humble and open mind is the best thing to have, so you should take on board whatever criticisms get thrown at you. Nope, that's a totally flawed social assumption and one I will explore in this chapter.

Listening to everyone, all the time, is not the key to thought leadership. There are times when you need to absent yourself from the well-meaning opinion of others. You need to free yourself from what others think and trust your own conviction. As thought leaders, there are times you will need to live by Terry Cole-Whittaker's mantra "What you think of me is none of my business." Or, in the words of the modern day poet Taylor Swift: "Haters gonna hate."

Get enough advice to improve your work, and not so much that it paralyses you from acting.

In his latest book *Four Seconds*, Peter Bregman explores some countercultural themes for getting things done. One idea that really struck a nerve with me is how often we look for feedback from the wrong people. His mum said "You don't go to a hardware store looking for milk." We often look for feedback from the wrong person, from the wrong perspective and at the wrong time as well.

Sometimes we look for feedback from the wrong people

I am not a big fan of constructive criticism, nor 360 degree feedback. These systems are based upon the assumption that everyone has a right to an opinion on you and your work. But if everyone was qualified to have an opinion on your work, shouldn't they be the ones doing it?

"Anonymous feedback is as useful as following a faceless leader."

— Georgia Murch, author of *Fixing Feedback*

Bregman recounts the time he was working on a TEDx talk and the effect people's suggestions had on his process. After countless revisions based upon the feedback of friends and colleagues, Bregman realised that he had lost his own voice in amongst a swathe of good advice. So he put that draft aside, and started again.

> "I looked through the thousands of words I had written in preparation for the talk to find something I felt added my unique perspective to the conversation. It seems obvious to me now, but how could I have hoped to find my unique perspective by asking others? Instead, I looked into the dark for what others had overlooked."

Crowdsourcing is a legitimate strategy for problem solving, but only in the right contexts. For example, studies have shown that by taking the average of hundreds or thousands of guesses, the crowd can very accurately guess "the number of jelly beans in the jar". There are times where the average is the optimum solution. Thought leadership is not an example of such a problem. We're not seeking average ideas, we're seeking ideas that challenge and stretch the status quo, and you won't achieve that by spouting back at the crowd something they already think. Sometimes, a great idea needs to be insulated from the crowd think.

So how do we decide what to do with the opinions of others? How do we know when, what and who to listen to?

If you are changing the world, making a difference or taking a stand, it's helpful to ask two questions (See Figure 32 on page 243):

1. Did I ask for this?

2. Are they qualified to have an opinion?

If the feedback was unsolicited and the giver doesn't have the expertise to hold that opinion, it's Noise. You should ignore it. You have little to gain and much to lose by investing effort in responding to this kind of feedback. It is more likely to detract from your work than improve it, and highly likely to derail your energy and motivation. Your thought leadership deserves to be held at arms length from the well-meaning interference of people whose major claim to fame is that they have an opinion. These people are often the most vocal and most passionate in their unasked for opinion. It's vital to learn how to shut this out.

If the feedback is unsolicited but the person has some expertise on the matter, then it's an Opinion, and worth considering. A failure to follow good etiquette in asking if you wanted an opinion should not make you instantly discount it. There are great opportunities to learn from experts around us, and someone may have noticed an area for you to improve that you weren't even aware of. Great! You may decide to take their feedback on board. Equally, you may decide not to follow it, or that it's not the right feedback for the time. You are completely within your rights to choose what you do with this feedback.

Listening to everyone, all the time, is not the key to thought leadership.

If the feedback is solicited but the person is not super qualified to hold the opinion, that's ok. It's Data. Just be aware that you are simply gathering information. It's a poll, a survey, a simple data collection point. Don't let this kind of feedback directly influence your great work. What it's doing is giving you more information, which you can then use to make your decision. You're looking for trends in the data rather than reading into individual responses. Prepare for these opinions with a conscious filtering process. We have experts for a reason, and some pieces of work are not suited to a general mindset.

If the feedback is solicited and the person is qualified to give it, it's Advice. In most cases, you're going to act on this. It's likely that it will improve your project, or finetune the details of what you're trying to communicate. Everyone should have a group of trusted advisors. Note though, that there's still a limit to how much is useful. Get enough advice to improve your work, and not so much that it paralyses you from acting.

QUALIFIED

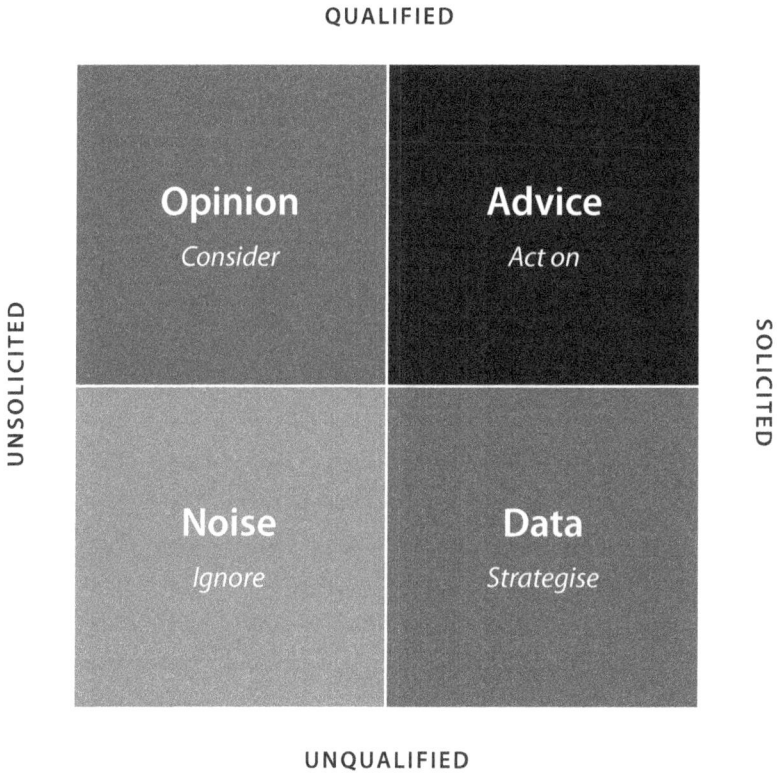

UNSOLICITED

SOLICITED

Opinion	Advice
Consider	*Act on*
Noise	Data
Ignore	*Strategise*

UNQUALIFIED

Figure 32.   When to listen to feedback

Sometimes we look for feedback from the wrong perspective

Imagine we experience feedback as we experience driving a car. You can use the rear-view mirror to see what's happening behind you, or the windscreen to see what's happening in front. I reckon the balance between the two is proportional to the actual size of each. When you drive you spend a little time looking back and a lot of time looking forward. This ratio is useful to remember when seeking out feedback for yourself.

Instead of the approach "Let's talk about what did not work", why not ask the question, "If we are faced with this situation again, what would you change?" When you step back through the history, people are more likely to take it personally and get offended. The conversation can often degenerate into a defence of past decisions made. When you focus on the future, however, people get to move into a creative space. The feedback suddenly become about inventing tomorrow instead of justifying yesterday.

Have you ever been driving behind someone slow, who is oblivious to the build up of frustrated traffic behind them? By failing to look in their rear-view mirror, they haven't noticed what's going on and are not able to resolve the situation. Equally, you don't pull out into traffic without checking your mirror to see what's behind you. You look backwards first, get the information you need, and then look forwards and drive on. You still need to look at your past. Just don't make it the only way you manage or handle feedback.

One of the exercises we use at Thought Leaders Business School is the 'Pre-mortem'. You imagine yourself at the end of the project you're embarking on, and you imagine it all went wrong. It's exercising hindsight in foresight. This gives you the ability to work through these problems before they've even happened. When seeking feedback, you're actually seeking hindsight in advance, from someone else's perspective. This can be a really useful tool.

Sometimes we look for feedback at the wrong time

The amount and type of feedback that we want varies enormously depending on what stage of an idea we're on. Getting the wrong type of feedback at the wrong time can slow down, stunt, or even completely shut down a project. Therefore, it's useful to consciously plan out when you're going to seek and accept feedback, and of what type. Here's a timeline that will give you a good starting point.

You still need to look at your past. Just don't make it the only way you manage or handle feedback.

IDEATE

Get lots of general input

The purpose of this stage is to sound out a new idea. You need to find out whether people are excited by it, and whether it has a decent chance of succeeding. Negative feedback at this stage may be disheartening, but remember, it's far better to find out the weaknesses of an idea now than down the track when you're launching. Be comfortable discussing the concept broadly and getting input from a range of sources. You may find that your idea becomes strengthened by robust discussion and by your repeated retelling of it.

INCUBATE

Reflect and talk to no one

Too much well intentioned advice too early and you lose your momentum. You've got all the input you needed in the previous stage. You've found out whether the idea, at a basic level, is likely to succeed. Now is the time to let your brain sort through the content, and decide what to do with it. Continuing to bounce your idea off anyone and everyone will just get you confused. Trust yourself to make your idea great from here.

ACTIVATE

Only discuss how to get it out there

There is no room for doubt when you're launching an idea, so it's important not to accept critical feedback at this stage. It cannot serve you in the moment. Too much negative feedback at this stage can induce paralysis, making you afraid of taking the actions to get the idea off the ground. The only feedback that's useful is feedback that helps you to deliver your idea better. You need to know how to get your idea out there, so seek out sources that can help you do this.

ITERATE

Specific targeted insights

At this stage we've delivered our idea, and it's now useful to find out how we could do it better next time. Being open to critical feedback here is useful to future projects, so be prepared to seek some out. Still remain clear though, on where this feedback should be targeted. We're only interested in feedback that will improve our ideas and delivery going forwards.

As a leader, you cannot afford to be at the mercy of those who want to give you feedback. Always remember that you are in control of what type of feedback you receive, who you receive it from, and at what time. By wisely shaping the feedback that comes your way, you'll not only create better ideas, but also maintain your own confidence and motivation.

BOOKS MENTIONED

Bregman, P., 2015. *Four Seconds: All the Time You Need to Stop Counter-Productive Habits and Get the Results You Want.* 1st ed. United States: HarperOne.

Murch, G., 2016. *Fixing Feedback.* 1st ed. Australia: John Wiley & Sons Australia, Ltd.

DISCUSSION IDEAS

1 Have a discussion with the people next to you around the idea of focusing on negative feedback only.

_____

_____

_____

2 Have you ever been in a 360 degree feedback discussion and felt attacked? If so, what made you feel like that?

_____

_____

_____

3 Have a discussion about the challenge of fitting in and standing out in a business.

_____

_____

_____

4 Should feedback be anonymous?

_____

_____

_____

5 If so, why? If not, why not?

_____

_____

_____

6 Are performance reviews useful?

_____

_____

_____

7 Do you look forward to them?

_____

_____

_____

8 Review fixed versus growth mindsets online
and determine how each mindset approaches
feedback. Have a discussion around your findings.

_____

_____

_____

COMMIT TO THE COMMITTED

How many summers do you have left? Sobering thought isn't it? This chapter explores the idea of living a life by design, not default. It challenges the social norms and poses the hypothetical idea of having achieved financial freedom and being at choice around your work. The idea that you do work you love with people you like the way you want. Great topic to finish on.

I imagined a few years back what it would be like to be retired, or more importantly, financially independent. Imagine that, through hard (smart) work and astute (consistent) investment, you had bought your time back. This exercise is less about money and more about how you might spend your time if this was true.

- *What would you do?*

- *What would you say yes to?*

- *And what would you say no to?*

- *Would you take that meeting?*

- *Would you continue to nurture that relationship or let it go?*

I decided that even though I was not near that goal at the time, I would act as if I was. I decided to be 'that', whether I had achieved it or not. This was less a social experiment and more a decision based on living a life by design, not default. It came after observing the way people were going out at night pretending they were networking and then proclaiming to want to spend more time with their kids.

Lex and the kids are my first priority, my health is second, and committing to the committed became my filter for how I would invest the rest of my time. That, and being on my boat floating ideas around.

As a result, I don't network to get ahead; I connect to inspire and be inspired. I rarely say yes to coffee catch ups and joint ventures. I don't respond to fast media requests for comment. And a meeting I do attend that doesn't progress something or advance a wildly important goal feels like a kind of robbery. I'll never get that 30 minutes back again. If I am not with Lex and the kids, then we better be doing something truly worthy of the time. It's got a certain ruthless quality to it and it no doubt offends or hurts many people in my life. Any offence is not intentional; I simply don't want to waste a minute doing something that is not something I choose fully. Lorna Patten, one of my coaches, once explained this as self-referring as opposed to self-centred — nice distinction.

Here is one of my standard responses to a request for a meeting:

Hey there,

I really appreciate you reaching out and trying to find a time to meet. Professionally I am super focussed right now on three things: the Thought Leaders Business School, my latest book and my Conference Keynote business.

I also made a choice a few years back that I would try to have it all. Family, loving relationships, deep friendships and a successful business. For this to all happen my schedule has become very compressed.

I am not taking on any new projects at this stage as I strive to deliver on my work life integration. So I am making sure that any meetings I do have are super productive and beneficial for all parties involved.

If, knowing this, you still want to meet then let's clarify what we can achieve together before we get together.

My business manager Sarah is the perfect person to discuss all this with and I have CC'd her in on our conversation.

I get that this means I can't be all things to all people, but for this little duck it's the key to focus and achieving everything I can in this busy time of life.

Thanks again for making a connection and reaching out.

Does this mean I'll miss an opportunity here or there? Absolutely, but FOMO (fear of missing out) is a concept born of lack, a scarcity idea, and one that distracts you from what you really want.

If you are truly at choice, what do you choose? I choose to commit to the committed. Not just those who share my blood, not just those who are in my orbit but those who turn up to put something

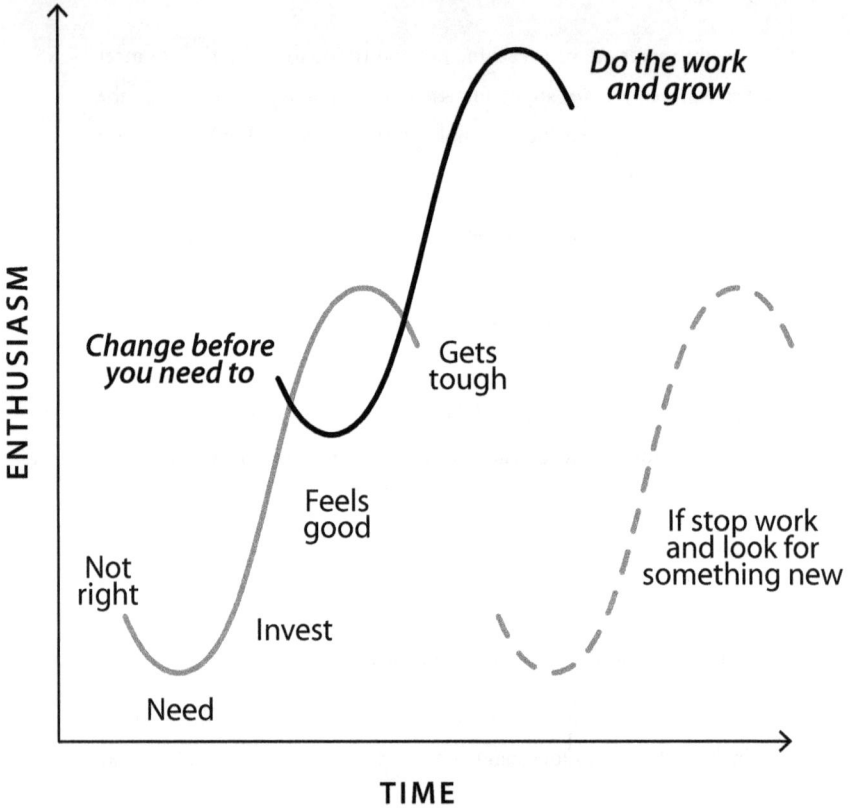

Figure 33. Serial commitment

into life, to make a difference, shake the tree, reject the status quo. For me, that group is thought leaders, people who dare to stick their head up, have an opinion and stand for something. What do you choose? Who do you choose?

So many procrastinators will hope a relationship with you gets their job done or their goal achieved. Don't spend time with them, it doesn't help them if you do their homework. People join gyms, go to self-help seminars, and buy books without turning up to exercise, applying an idea, or turning a page. Interested is not committed.

Interested is not committed.

I have learnt from years of running leadership and personal development programs that for some people, investing in the course is the commitment. It's like joining a gym but never actually turning up to train. The real commitment is not the payment or enrolment in a program, it's doing the work. When the going gets tough (and it always does), some people enrol in a new course, hopping from one program to the next. Figure 33 on page 255 shows you the pattern.

There is a great video by Scott Belsky, founder of Behance and author of *Making Ideas Happen*, which walks you through this idea from a creativity perspective.[1]

It's never about the money, but money is a good start. Money is the lowest form of commitment. Doing the work is what we need to stay focused on if we want to reap the rewards of our investment. The commitment ladder has money at the bottom, time next, then energy (the last two being the work), and finally identity (see Figure 34 on page 256).

Thought Leaders Business School helps experts improve the financial performance of their consulting practice. Occasionally a student gets through the enrolment process with a 'this will fix it for me' mindset, when in reality only they can do the work required.

Identity *Character*	When it becomes who you are and what you do. You can't imagine not sticking at it.
Energy *Intensity*	Turning up is fine. Putting in, getting better results than mere attendance.
Time *Frequency*	You have to turn up. Sometimes that's all it takes to progress.
Money *Decision*	We know that often the 'free' is less valued. Putting skin in the game is a good start.

Figure 34.   The ladder of commitment

You simply can't buy the result, you need to do the work. You can't outsource commitment.

So if you did not have to work, what would you do differently?

It's a great question and one that business and life coaches like to throw around with abandon. It's worth the risk of cynical disdain to ask it here, so really 'If you did not have to work, what would you do differently?'

This question is sneaky because it's less about work and retirement or financial independence and more about life on your terms. It's what my business partner Pete calls a 'life without compromise'.

What they think of you is none of your business.

Be clear on what you say no to, that way you have the capacity for the things you want to say yes to. It's a place where you can begin to live a life by design, not default.

- **Get good at saying no.** Commit carefully and less often.

- **Don't do other's work for them.** It's disempowering for them and builds resentment in you.

- **Don't try to please everyone.** Just accept that some will and some won't. And that what they think of you is none of your business.

- **Obsess about leverage.** Resist the status quo. There is always the possibility that there is a faster, smarter, or better way to do things than how it's been done to date.

- **Get really clear about what matters most to you.** You only have X summers ahead of you, don't waste them in obligation, desperation, or compromise.

We don't say no for a bunch of reasons but really for me I say no to the things that don't align so that I can say yes to what matters. Make this the week of no and see what happens. My friend Rowdy

McLean, author of *Play a Bigger Game,* once did a year of saying no. I learnt so much around this idea watching him work and live without compromise. Compassionate, considerate, generous, and focussed on making sure he did the things that mattered most, not the things we often feel obliged to do. Interestingly, he had more time for people who would not normally ask for time and less for those he might not normally choose to help. The squeaky wheels did not get the most attention.

COUNTERPOINT

My biggest counterpoint to this is to be very clear that you can't be efficient with relationships. If your old dad needs to spend 10 minutes or so talking through the exhaust problem on his 1962 converted trawler (hypothetically), then it's OK. It's not about the trawler, it's about his desire to be grounded in something real. In this case to bring back to life something honest and true rather than bob around on a show-off plastic mid-life crisis. It's about his desire to share that we should have a fix-it-up society, not the planned obsolescence mindset that's in most things today and leading to landfill.

Don't cut corners with the meaningful relationships in your life — they deserve genuine attention and time.

ONLINE REFERENCES

1. Scott Belsky, *How To Avoid The Idea Generation Trap - 99U*. http://99u.com/videos/6701/scott-belsky-how-to-avoid-the-idea-generation-trap

BOOKS MENTIONED

McLean, R., 2012. *Play A Bigger Game!: Achieve More! Be More! Do More! Have More!*. 1st ed. Australia: John Wiley & Sons Australia, Ltd.

DISCUSSION IDEAS

1 Can you think of a time where instead of staying
committed you switched to a new idea?

_____

_____

_____

2 Are you a good finisher?

_____

_____

_____

3 Or are you a serial starter?

_____

_____

_____

4 What do you commit to?

_____

_____

_____

5 Who are you committed to?

_____

_____

_____

6 Where have you said 'no' in the past and its backfired?

_____

_____

_____

7 Where have you said 'no' in the past and its helped?

_____

_____

_____

8 Why stops you saying 'no'?

_____

_____

_____

9 Whats your 'work you love'?

_____

_____

_____

10 Whats your 'people you like'?

_____

_____

_____

11 What does 'the way you want' look like for you?

_____

_____

_____